Purchased with funds from the
Wyoming Community Foundation
McMurry Library Endowment.

TREE BARK

TREE
BARK

A COLOR GUIDE

by

HUGUES VAUCHER

translated and edited by

JAMES E. ECKENWALDER

TIMBER PRESS
Portland · Cambridge

All photographs by Hugues Vaucher except those in Chapter 2 and that of *Wollemia* in Chapter 4; page 2, *Betula papyrifera*, paper birch, photographed in the Kalmthout Arboretum, Belgium; page 11, *Prunus serrula*, birch-bark cherry, photographed in the Van Dusen Botanical Garden, Vancouver, Canada; page 21, *Eucalyptus delegatensis*, woolly butt, photographed in Mount Usher Gardens, Ireland; page 39, *Pinus sylvestris*, Scots pine, photographed at Fernhill Garden, Ireland; page 51, *Quercus robur*, English oak, photographed on the Swiss Plateau.

Translated, and revised and enlarged, from *Guide des écorces*, published in 1993, which was published in 1990 as *Baumrinden*.

Published in 2003 by

Timber Press, Inc.
The Haseltine Building
133 S.W. Second Avenue, Suite 450
Portland, Oregon 97204, U.S.A.

Timber Press
2 Station Road
Swavesey
Cambridge CB4 5QJ, U.K.

Printed in Hong Kong
Designed by Susan Applegate

Library of Congress Cataloging-in-Publication Data

Vaucher, Hugues, 1922–
 [Guide des écorces]
 Tree bark: a color guide / Hugues Vaucher; translated and edited by James E. Eckenwalder.
  p. cm.
 Includes bibliographical references (p.   ).
 ISBN 0-88192-576-4
  1. Bark. 2. Bark—Pictorial works. 3. Trees—Pictorial works. I. Eckenwalder, James E., 1949– II. Title.

QK648.V3913 2003
582.16—dc21   2002029148

CONTENTS

FOREWORD

THIS TREATISE, on the diversity to be found in tree bark, covers a subject hitherto rarely addressed. Although quite conspicuous and essential for the protection of the tree, bark has been much less studied than wood. This book treats the kinds of barks, their structures, functions, characteristics, and finally, their uses in the arts and industry.

The text and illustrations allow one to better understand tree physiology, to learn to identify trees by their bark, and to learn how bark is used, for example, as a source of energy, a substitute for peat, a raw material for making particle board, for cork products, or as extractives for phytomedicines.

More than 550 magnificent color photographs illustrate the barks. The wealth of textures reveals the beauty of their varying themes, which are too often ignored. The species selected cover a broad spectrum of trees found within the temperate and subtropical zones. The many photographs of bark result from the keen enthusiasm the author has for the subject. He has devoted many years to searching out typical and unusual examples, and his pleasure in close observation of tree trunks reveals to us a world of patterns and structure that only nature can offer.

One hopes that this book will reach a wider audience than just professionals involved with trees. All friends of nature as well as those who love trees will open their eyes with new appreciation after they have read this book, which unveils the secrets and the infinite variety of the "clothing" of trees.

DR. THEO HEGETSCHWEILER
Honorary President
Swiss Dendrological Society

PREFACE

THEORETICALLY, it would take at least a million pictures to cover the full variety of textures found in tree barks. There are more than 60,000 woody plants in the world, among which some 10,000 species can certainly be considered trees. If one were to photograph trunks of each species at 10 different localities and at 10 different stages of growth, the result would be 100 photographs multiplied by 10,000 species, that is, a million. A bit more realistically, one could restrict oneself to just 1000 well-known tree species and take only 10 photographs per species instead of 100. This would still mean taking 10,000 pictures, filling many large-format volumes.

For practical reasons it was necessary to be selective, and I have included more than 550 photographs to illustrate the polymorphism of bark, embracing more than 440 species and varieties of trees. The selection of species was not strictly the result of systematic planning but the result of discoveries made during pleasant walks through the forest, visits to parks and gardens, and dendrological excursions, as reflected in the localities given in the captions. Species from around the world are included, but trees native to Europe as well as those from temperate North America and eastern Asia are most richly represented. I must emphasize that each illustration shows just one example of the possible textures and that nature has many means to vary the form and color of the bark of an individual tree or single species.

The field of exploration and research within the realm of bark texture lies wide open to any photographer, amateur or expert, who wishes to make it his or her pastime. One has only to look at bark closely for it to become interesting—even obsessing, otherwise this book would never have seen the light of day!

ACKNOWLEDGMENTS

For their collaboration in writing the original version of this work, I very sincerely thank the following:

Prof. Dr. Ladislav J. Kučera and Dr. Livia Bergamin of the Forest and Wood Research Institute, Swiss Federal Institute of Technology, Zürich, for Chapter 2 and the accompanying photomicrographs of bark structure

PD Dr. sci. nat. Beat Meier, Zeller AG, Plant Remedies, Romanshorn, for the section, Bark in Phytotherapy, in Chapter 3

Martine Guex for the drawings of bark in Chapter 1

Ursula Stocker of the Forest and Wood Research Institute for the diagrams of stem anatomy in Chapter 2

Sabine Süsstrunk of the Institute for Communications Technology, Swiss Federal Institute of Technology, for the photographs of stem sections (Figures 5–16) in Chapter 2

CHAPTER 1
THE DIVERSITY
OF BARK

Anything becomes interesting when you look at it closely.
Eugenio d'Ors
1882–1954

THE CASUAL STROLLER will see all tree trunks as similar, often dull, monotonous, uniform, and without any special charm. In contrast, an observer who takes the time to look closely, comparing and touching, will see the infinite variety hidden in the patterns, colors, and textures of tree bark. If the passerby is an inquisitive artist or an eager seeker of discoveries, he or she will very quickly be drawn to the natural beauty of bark. The visual sensations provoked by natural and harmonious patterns such as those of tree bark can inspire the creation of ornaments and artwork. So tree bark merits more than just a fleeting glance in passing. If the walker is a naturalist who loves trees, it is enough to look closely to see that bark is interesting. Unlocking the secrets contained in bark becomes a challenge, a game, trying to recognize trees by their bark.

Each species of tree is relatively easy to identify if you carefully examine its silhouette, its trunk and branches, its buds or flowers, and above all, its leaves. But to recognize a tree just by looking at its bark alone is not an easy task. As far as I know, there is no key for identifying species of trees by their bark characteristics. Although it is easy to distinguish an oak from a birch or a chestnut, it is much harder, sometimes impossible, to separate the various species of oaks, birches, or chestnuts by just their barks.

From its first year right up to the death of the tree, bark undergoes a long development that changes it through the years. The bark is transformed by the growth of the trunk. This alteration is conditioned by the internal state and age of the tree itself, the composition and quality of the soil, the moisture regime, the climate, the amount of sunshine, the geographical site and elevation, the local environment (whether in a forest or standing alone), disease, and the influence of animals and of the microflora. Identification must thus take into account a host of complicating factors in order to determine a species, methodically and with certainty, on the basis of the structure of its bark. In the end, practical experience based on observation and comparison of different barks remains the best guarantee of identification when leaves are lacking.

THE TYPES OF BARK

In order to learn what to look for in bark and to facilitate the recognition of tree species, here is an arbitrary classification of bark texture, divided into 18 different types, with examples drawn from the species illustrated in Chapter 4. Never forget, however, that an infinite variety occurs in nature and that the age of the tree plays a preeminent role in the form of its bark. As a consequence, a single tree may be assigned to different bark types throughout its life and may also possess bark at any one time that combines the characteristics of two or more types. Types 1–9 embrace barks that are firmly attached to the trunk. Types 10–14 include barks that peel away from the surface of the trunk. Types 15 and 16 have prominent lenticels, and types 17 and 18 are spiny.

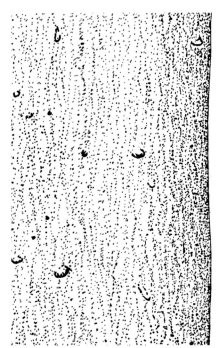 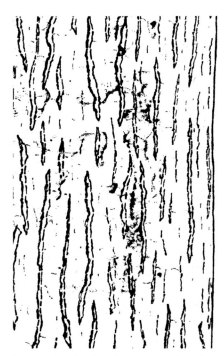

Type 1. Bark smooth, bumpy, or sometimes wrinkled; thin. Examples: *Carpinus betulus, Fagus sylvatica, Ilex aquifolium, Sorbus aria.*

Type 2. Bark with shallow, vertical fissures or ribs, or sometimes cracked; thin. Examples: *Acer capillipes, A. davidii, Cercis racemosa, Liriodendron tulipifera.*

Type 3. Bark with deep, vertical furrows and well-developed ridges that are sometimes wavy or curved; thick. Examples: *Castanea sativa, Liquidambar styraciflua, Quercus alba, Q. robur.*

Type 4. Bark with interlacing ridges; thick and hard. Examples: *Fraxinus excelsior, Juglans ×intermedia, Populus ×canadensis, Tilia cordata.*

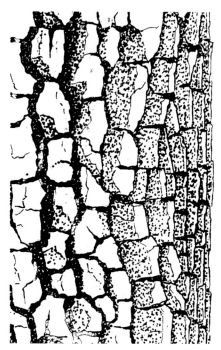

Type 5. Bark divided into square or rectangular blocks by deep fissures; thick and hard. Examples: *Diospyros kaki, D. virginiana, Ehretia dicksonii, Quercus garryana.*

Type 6. Corky bark with raised rhytidomes; thick and hard. Examples: *Casuarina torulosa, Phellodendron amurense, Quercus suber.*

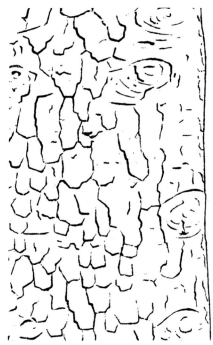

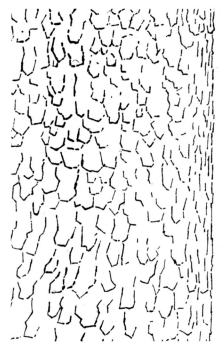

Type 7. Shallowly cracked bark with irregular scales; thin. Examples: *Abies alba, A. cephalonica, Cedrus libani* subsp. *atlantica, Pinus monticola.*

Type 8. Cracked bark with small to medium-sized scales; moderately thickened. Examples: *Ostrya japonica, Picea abies, Prunus serotina, Pyrus communis.*

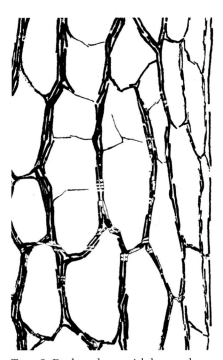

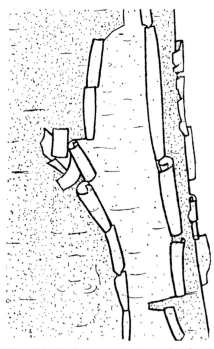

Type 9. Bark scaly or with large, elongated, asymmetrical plates; generally thick. Examples: *Pinus canariensis, P. halepensis, P. pinaster, P. pinea, P. sylvestris.*

Type 10. Bark separating into thin layers, rolling up in strips along the trunk and afterward flaking away; thin. Examples: *Acer griseum, A. triflorum, Betula maximowicziana, Platanus racemosa, Schinus molle.*

Type 11. Bark smooth or grainy but breaking up and flaking in asymmetrical patches, revealing lighter bark beneath; thin. Examples: *Lagerstroemia indica, Parrotia persica, Pinus bungeana, Platanus ×acerifolia, Pseudocydonia sinensis.*

Type 12. Bark fibrous or peeling in flexible, narrow strips; moderately thick. Examples: *Cryptomeria japonica, Cupressus nootkatensis, Juniperus chinensis, Metasequoia glyptostroboides, Thuja standishii.*

Type 13. Bark of rigid, rough, elongated plates or platelets that remain attached at one end after peeling; moderately thick. Examples: *Calocedrus decurrens, Carya laciniosa, C. ovata, Chamaecyparis lawsoniana.*

Type 14. Bark spongy, fibrous, broken up into longitudinal ridges that weather on top; relatively soft and often very thick. Examples: *Eucalyptus microcorys, Pseudotsuga menziesii, Sequoia sempervirens, Sequoiadendron giganteum, Taxodium distichum.*

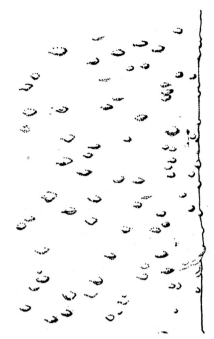

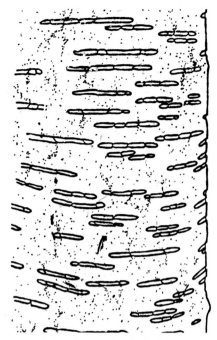

Type 15. Bark with scattered lenticels; thin. Examples: *Idesia polycarpa, Laburnum anagyroides, Pyrus ussuriensis, Sorbus latifolia.*

Type 16. Bark with lenticels forming horizontal lines; thin. Examples: *Betula lenta, Prunus avium, P. serrula, P. serrulata.*

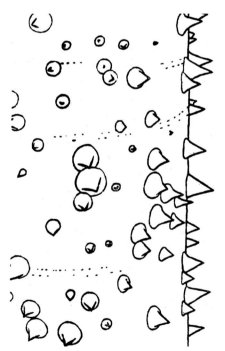

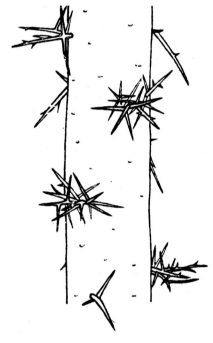

Type 17. Bark with thick, conical spines; thin. Examples: *Alluaudia* sp., *Chorisia speciosa, Erythrina velutina.*

Type 18. Bark with slender spines, often branched; thin. Examples: *Bactris* cf. *gasipaes, Gleditsia japonica, G. triacanthos, Pachypodium geayi, Pereskia grandifolia.*

SOME DECORATIVE BARKS

For readers who wish to use bark to its best advantage in the garden, here is a short list of trees with particularly attractive and decorative barks. As well as paying attention to climatic and soil conditions when choosing trees, you may get useful advice from a professional on specimen trees with captivating barks that you might wish to have in your garden.

Abies squamata
Acer, many species and varieties
Arbutus, some species and varieties
Betula, many species and varieties
Carya ovata
Cornus alba 'Sibirica'
Eucalyptus, many species and varieties
Firmiana simplex
Juniperus deppeana
Lagerstroemia indica
Luma apiculata

Parrotia persica
Pinus bungeana
Pinus halepensis
Platanus ×acerifolia
Prunus canescens × P. serrula
Prunus maackii
Prunus serrula
Prunus serrulata
Pseudocydonia sinensis
Pyrus ussuriensis
Stewartia pseudocamellia

CONCLUSION

The bark of a tree is as individual as a fingerprint. Although there may be other barks that resemble it, none will be identical. The polymorphism of barks—their variety in texture and color—is a curiosity of nature. One has to admire this diversity, a source of inspiration for artists and designers.

However, some barks are subject to the hazards of nature—fire, snow, and frost—each of which may alter or damage a bark's structure and function. The damage wrought by beetles, other animals, and fungi (and even mosses and lichens when they grow in heavy masses) sometimes causes the decline and death of trees. For their part, people are also unfortunately at the root of ill treatments meted out upon trees: arson, acid rain, air pollution, carved pictures and initials, and accidental or deliberate mechanical wounds. All upset the smooth functioning and normal growth of trees, which lack defenses against such aggression.

Although the patterns and colors of bark cannot compare with the beauty of flowers or the sparkling of precious stones and minerals, anyone who takes the time to examine bark closely will make discoveries that will as surely be a feast for the eyes. In nature, nothing is commonplace!

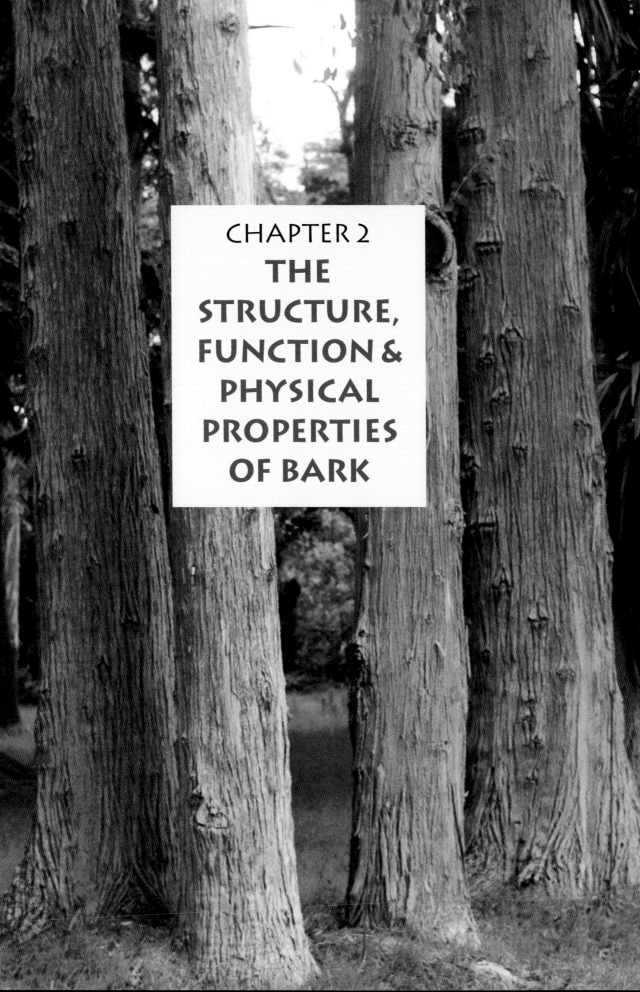

CHAPTER 2
THE STRUCTURE, FUNCTION & PHYSICAL PROPERTIES OF BARK

by **Ladislav J. Kučera and Livia Bergamin**

K NOWLEDGE OF THE structure and properties of bark is important for four reasons: (1) understanding the physiology of trees, (2) identifying a species on the basis of its bark, (3) evaluating a bark's usefulness and economic potential, and (4) interpreting the causes of disease and abnormality. The benefits of such knowledge underline the importance of studying bark for biologists, foresters, wood technologists, and indeed, anyone interested in knowing more about trees.

The bark, a protective layer completely enveloping the trunk, branches, and roots of a tree, has been the subject of far fewer studies than the wood, which it surrounds. There are two main reasons for this, one rather economic on the whole, the second arising from the methods used to study bark. The economic value of bark is both quantitatively and qualitatively less than that of wood. There is only about 10% as much bark as wood in an average stem. Furthermore, the physical properties of bark, such as stability and tensile strength, are characterized by much lower values than those of wood. The yield of heat (thermal gain) during combustion is about the same, but the numerous chemical compounds deposited in bark can be a source of environmental pollution. These compounds require special precautions for workplace safety, and the crystals that are frequently present significantly shorten the useful life of any tools used in working bark.

With respect to methods of investigation, the study of bark is a difficult and demanding undertaking. A specialized vocabulary has built up to describe the various aspects of bark, and the Glossary provides additional information on this terminology. The process of bark formation is much more complex than that of wood, and the structure of bark is more variable. Thus, for example, two different meristematic tissues (the vascular cambium and the cork cambium or phellogen) participate in the formation of bark whereas only the vascular cambium contributes to wood. Furthermore, bark is exposed to external factors from the onset of its formation (weather, injuries, and diseases) such that its appearance changes constantly as a result of wear and tear. Moreover, it is very difficult to determine the annual growth rate of bark because, unlike wood, there are no definite growth rings, or when they are present, the rings are narrow (less than 1 mm).

The Function of Bark

Although bark may seem to have little economic significance, it is of enormous importance to the tree because it protects it from external threats, both physical and biological. Because of the protection that bark affords, rain, snow, and hail (not to mention heat, frost, and ultraviolet rays) cannot reach and damage the soft and vulnerable vascular cambium. This physicochemical barrier is also difficult for animals (such as insects, birds, and mammals) and other living things (including parasitic plants, fungi, and bacteria) to penetrate. Besides this important protective role, bark has at least two supplementary functions. It serves as a dumping ground in which the tree can rid itself of waste products from its metabolism in the form of crystals, tannins, gums, or resins, by depositing them in zones that are about to die. On the other hand, large quantities of nutritious substances are transported within the living tissues (phloem) of the bark. With the rising of the sap in the spring, these nutrient reserves are transported from the roots to the crown. A little later, the direction shifts and the assimilates produced during photosynthesis circulate through the whole tree to nourish the growth of new tissues. Later, in the autumn, these substances no longer feed growth but are stored as reserves.

The Formation of Bark

DEVELOPMENT THROUGH GEOLOGICAL TIME

During the Carboniferous period, about 200–300 million years ago, there were immense forests spread across the land, with the first trees large and stately. They reached a diameter of 2 m (6½ feet) and a height of 40 m (130 feet), and their bark was extremely thick, making up about 90% of the cross section of the trunk. Unlike today's trees, the meristem that formed the bark was much more active, and most cells were produced toward the inside. Furthermore, the shape of the cells in the conducting tissues has evolved over the course of millions of years, changing from elongate with a narrow lumen to more or less square with a wider lumen.

DEVELOPMENT OF THE INDIVIDUAL TREE

During the course of development, secondary tissues (Figure 2) are added to the primary structures (epidermis; cortex, primary bark; and vascular bundles) found in the young dicotyledon (hardwood) twig (Figure 1). In comparison to the primary tissues, the secondary tissues become progressively more dominant in volume as the stem thickens.

The vascular cambium, in forming secondary tissues, produces bast (secondary phloem) toward the outside and wood (secondary xylem) toward the inside. At the same time, the cortex continues to develop, and a second tissue capable of cell division, the cork cambium (or phellogen), differentiates among the living cells of its parenchymatous tissue. The cork cambium produces cork (phellem) toward the outside and phelloderm toward the inside. These three tissues together are referred to as initial periderm. The initial periderm can have a long life—60 years or more in silver firs (*Abies alba*), birches (*Betula*), and spruces (*Picea*)—or a short one (just a few years in the majority of other temperate trees). If the life span is short, the initial periderm dies after a while and a new periderm, a secondary periderm, just as capable of cell division, is organized within the inner bark out of living parenchyma cells. This periderm can either encircle the entire trunk (continuous periderm, Figure 3) or take the form of discrete wedges (lenticular periderm, Figure 4.)

STRUCTURE OF THE BAST

The bast (or secondary phloem) is an assemblage of tissues produced by the vascular cambium toward the outside (Figures 3 and 4). It serves primarily for the vertical and horizontal transport of assimilates (sugars and amino acids). It conveys the products of photosynthesis from the leaves where they are formed to the meristems where they are used. In conformity with this function, the bast consists mostly of sieve elements, so named because their end walls are perforated like a sieve. In conifers, the sieve elements are called sieve cells and the perforations are called sieve areas. In the hardwoods, the cells that transport assimilates are referred to as sieve tube elements and the end walls are called sieve plates. Both sieve areas and sieve plates contain sieve pores, tiny channels linking adjacent sieve elements to one another.

Sieve elements, which often lack a cell nucleus, are living cells that are nourished by the adjoining companion cells or by parenchyma cells. The soft bast is made up of these three thin-walled cell types. The parenchymatous storage tissue is composed of radial (horizontal) phloem rays and axial (vertical) phloem parenchyma. The hard bast is made up primarily of phloem fibers, elongate cells with thick walls. Because of their strength, they are used to make fabrics such as linen, hemp, and ramie. The firmness of the bast is the result of its sclerenchyma. This tissue is composed of sclerenchyma fibers (also called phloem fibers), formed directly by the vascular cambium, and of sclereids (also called stone cells), which can take different forms. The sclereids are derived from parenchyma cells that have undergone enlargement and a thickening of the cell wall. Sclereids are found primarily in the outer layers of the bast after these have lost their capacity to function actively.

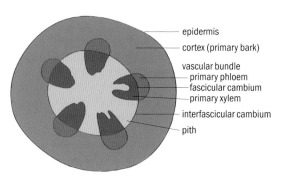

Figure 1. Diagram of the primary structure of a hardwood twig, in transverse (cross) section.

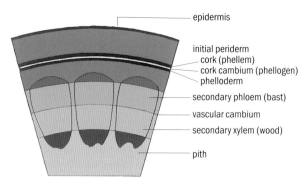

Figure 2. Diagram of the secondary structure of a hardwood twig at the end of the first year, in transverse section.

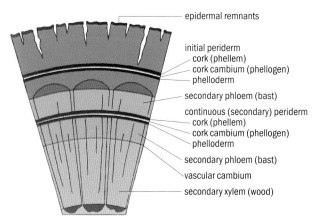

Figure 3. Diagram of the tissues in a young trunk with continuous periderm, in transverse section.

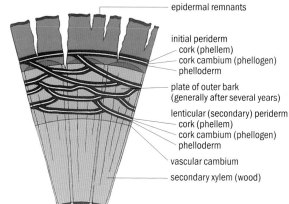

Figure 4. Diagram of the tissues in a young trunk with lenticular periderm, in transverse section.

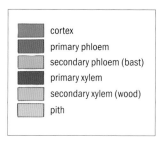

26

Comparison of phloem and xylem elements

FUNCTION	PHLOEM (elements of the bast)	XYLEM (elements of the wood)
Transport	Sieve cells or sieve tube elements	Tracheids and vessels
Functional control of the sieve elements	Companion cells	—
Accumulation and synthesis of secondary compounds	Parenchyma cells in the rays and the phloem parenchyma	Parenchyma cells in the wood rays and in the wood parenchyma
Support	Phloem fibers and sclereids	Wood (libriform) fibers and tracheids

The secondary phloem of temperate trees is rather scanty in comparison to the secondary xylem: it can be between 0.3 mm (European dogwood, *Cornus sanguinea*) and 14 mm (½ inch) thick (European beech, *Fagus sylvatica*). Expressed as a percentage, the relative thickness of the bark of traveler's joy (*Clematis vitalba*) makes up about 10% of the radius of a 5-year-old shoot whereas that of an oak 470 years old is only about 1%. One can sometimes make out regular structures in the bast that look like annual rings but are not. These arise from the successive alternation of hard bast and soft bast. A few trees, nevertheless, form true rings in the phloem, the vascular cambium producing cells both to the outside and to the inside with an annual rhythm. When present, these rings are more distinct in conifers than in hardwoods. Furthermore, one can see zones of early bast and of late bast within these rings, just as in wood.

FORMATION OF THE OUTER BARK

The primary function of the outer bark (rhytidome) is to protect the tree. It is made up of dead layers. The first cork cambium ceases to divide after a while and then differentiates. Within the living tissue layers of the phloem lying underneath, a new cork cambium arises that will, in turn, cease dividing, and so on. In the outer part of the newly formed periderm, the cells deposit suberin in their walls, creating an isolating layer that is impermeable to water, and then die. In this way, new layers keep forming and the rhytidome thickens bit by bit. If the periderms are concentric, they produce an annular rhytidome that peels away from the trunk in strings or in strips. This rhytidome is not really thick at first (Figure 3). Japanese redwood (*Cryptomeria japonica*), common juniper (*Juniperus communis*), and traveler's joy (*Clematis vitalba*) are examples of woody plants with an annular rhytidome. If the periderms are arranged in the form of scales, one speaks of a scaly rhytidome (Figure 4). This type can form impressive barks that, over time, flake away, scale by scale. This is the type of bark found most commonly in temperate trees. Some familiar examples are European larch (*Larix decidua*), English oak (*Quercus robur*), and Norway spruce (*Picea abies*). There are some rare cases in which the first cork cambium remains active and no secondary periderms are produced, so that there is no rhytidome in the strict sense. European beech (*Fagus sylvatica*) and cork oak (*Q. suber*) are examples of trees with a long-lived first cork cambium. The form of the outer bark is characteristic for each species. Its outward appearance depends on numerous external conditions (such as climate and growth) and internal factors (type of periderm and composition of the phloem) and thus varies tremendously. We can distinguish the following types of outer bark in the trees of middle latitudes:

Annular rhytidome. Outer bark produced by a continuous (or annular) periderm and that peels away from the bark in strings or strips; for example, northern white cedar (*Thuja occidentalis*), common juniper (*Juniperus communis*), and traveler's joy (*Clematis vitalba*)

Scaly rhytidome. Outer bark produced by lenticular (or scaly) periderm

Fibrous subtype. High proportion of fibers and peeling away in strips; for example, common linden (*Tilia ×vulgaris*), European ash (*Fraxinus excelsior*), and Norway maple (*Acer platanoides*)

Flaky subtype. Many sclereids and peeling away in flakes; for example, European larch (*Larix decidua*) and sycamore maple (*Acer pseudoplatanus*)

The cork cambium (phellogen) produces cork (phellem) toward the outside and, toward the inside, phelloderm, a layer of living parenchyma cells that is usually rather scanty. The cork is composed of three types of corky cells, which are variously suberized (containing more or less suberin): (1) hollow cork cells with thin walls that provide a zone of weakness at which pieces of rhytidome can flake away, (2) stony cork cells with thick walls that are responsible for waterproofing, and (3) phlobaphene-containing cork cells that sequester tannin-like substances and protect against mechanical injury.

In order for gas exchange to take place between the atmosphere and the internal living tissues across the rhytidome, lenticels (corky outgrowths) develop within the new periderm under the old stomata. The lenticels are built up of loosely layered filling cells (or complementary cells) produced by the cork cambium that, over time, rupture the tissues under which they lie. Their intercellular spaces allow unimpeded gas exchange.

Many trees also have cork bands along the length of the stem. These form either by increased production of cork (such as the true cork bands in winged spindle tree, *Euonymus alatus*) or by shredding of the rhytidome (such as the false cork bands in field maple, *Acer campestre*).

Many tropical trees, particularly those with a palm-like growth habit consisting of a tuft of large leaves at the top of a stout, unbranched stem, lack ordinary secondary growth and thus may not follow the patterns of bark formation just described. The bark of these trees forms by a variety of different processes, but two patterns involving organs in addition to the trunk are prevalent. Most often, portions of the leaf bases remain and help protect the trunk after the leaf blade and stalk have been shed. The amount of leaf tissue left behind varies greatly. In some species, like Chilean wine palm (*Jubaea chilensis*) or coconut palm (*Cocos nucifera*), the leaves are shed cleanly and special periderms are associated with the resulting leaf scars. At the other extreme, exemplified by some species of *Yucca* such as narrow-leaf yucca (*Y. angustissima*), the whole leaf shrivels and is retained, forming a dense thatch. In between are species with prominent leaf base remnants, like date palm (*Phoenix dactylifera*) or Australian rough tree fern (*Cyathea australis*). Many palm trees, including date palm, also retain a dense thatch of fibers that are associated with the leaf bases. Besides leaf bases, the other organs that commonly help to protect trunks in these anomalous trees, particularly near the base, are adventitious roots that grow out from the trunk well above ground level. These roots grow tightly massed and are often cemented together by secretions to form a solid bark layer. Such roots are found in many tree ferns and some palms, such as date palm. The whole world's tally of these trees with anomalous bark formation represents just a tiny portion of all tree species, no more that 5%. (This paragraph is added by the translator to accommodate the trees added to the English edition.)

MATURATION OF BARK

The aging of bark results in obvious changes in appearance, unlike wood, which changes very little during the course of the life of the tree. The aging process is driven by both physical and physiological causes. After the formation of new conducting tissues, the old ones cease their activities after a while and fill up with waste products. The death of the tissues and the storage of substances within them happen at different times, and the exact order is unknown in most cases. The sieve elements of the bast are blocked with callose and thus cease functioning. Following this, the nearby parenchyma cells swell up, and this usually leads to the collapse of the sieve elements. The sequestering of excess metabolites takes place in special parenchyma cells called idioblasts. The stored substances can include resins (*Pinus*), mucilage (*Ulmus*), tannins (*Quercus, Betula, Salix,* and *Picea*), or crystals (*Tilia* and *Fagus*). Whereas resins, mucilage, and tannins are mixtures of materials, the crystals are composed primarily of calcium oxalate or of silicates. In addition to these physiological processes, there are physical causes for aging, as mentioned. As a result of the stresses in bark caused by its constant growth, the inner parts are under compression while the outer ones are subject to tension.

The living cells of the inner bark react to radial compression by sclerification (thickening of the cell wall), which increases the rigidity of the tissue as a whole. Those trees with a thin bark, for example, beech (*Fagus*), often have zones that are strongly sclerified. The form, frequency, color, and arrangement of these zones in cross section are important features in identifying tree species by their bark. These features, furthermore, give an indication of the quality of the site for tree growth. For example, Norway spruce (*Picea abies*), when growing on good sites, has zones of bark that are less sclerified overall than when it grows on poor soil.

As growth in thickness continues, the outer layers of the bark are under tension because of tangential stretching. This causes minute tears in the tissue, which the trees have two ways of repairing. In some trees, the cells begin to divide and fill in the gaps by profuse growth (dilatation), as they do in common linden (*Tilia ×vulgaris*). Other trees, for example, conifers, oaks (*Quercus*), and maples (*Acer*), produce new periderms from which the rhytidome forms, as described. It is also possible for dilatation and the formation of secondary periderms to be combined.

Bark thickness of some trees

LATIN NAME	ENGLISH NAME	BARK THICKNESS (mm)
CONIFERS		
Juniperus	juniper	2–6
Larix	larch	5–50
Picea	spruce	5–30
Pinus	pine	5–50
Pseudotsuga	Douglas fir	2–10
Thuja	arborvitae, cedar	2–6
HARDWOODS		
Acer	maple	5–20
Betula	birch	5–30
Fagus	beech	2–10
Populus	poplar	5–80
Quercus	oak	5–40
Robinia	black locust	5–60
Tilia	linden, basswood	5–20
Ulmus	elm	5–30

Physical Properties of Bark

The physicochemical properties of barks determine how they have been used in different societies throughout the ages. Today, it is increasingly important to think about recycling and other ways to protect the environment since bark makes up 6–22% as much of the bulk of the trunk as the wood. In many lumber mills, bark has often been discarded as waste or burned in the open air. This poses a big problem in terms of groundwater contamination and air pollution and is the reason that, in addition to traditional markets, new uses are being developed for bark, such as composting, chipping, biological insulation of buildings, and animal bedding. The exploitation of bark takes advantage of its three most important properties: its energy content, which is about the same as that of wood; its low density; and the diverse cellular contents. The heat content of dry bark is approximately 18,000 kilojoules per kilogram (kJ/kg), practically the same as completely dry wood. The density is about 350 kilograms per cubic meter (kg/m^3) of dry bark, about in the midrange of that of wood. Its low weight and the somewhat increased proportion of fibers make bark an interesting material for insulation. These physical properties and the high concentration of chemical cell contents explain the diverse potential uses for bark. This subject is explored further in Chapter 3.

Physical properties of barks*

LATIN NAME	DENSITY (kg/m^3)	HEAT CONTENT (kJ/kg)	ASH CONTENT (%)	WATER CONTENT (%)	BARK PRO- PORTION (%)
CONIFERS					
Abies alba	—	19,080	2.6	—	11–12
Abies balsamea	380	—	2.3	—	—
Larix decidua	—	19,800	1.2	—	16–22
Larix laricina	280	20,850	—	—	—
Picea abies	—	18,930	3.3	—	—
Picea sp.	420	—	—	55–80	—
Pinus contorta	—	25,050	2.0	—	—
Pinus sylvestris	—	20,160	1.5	—	—
Pinus sp.	340	—	—	43–143	—
Pseudotsuga menziesii	500	—	—	28–135	—
Thuja plicata	340	—	—	105–125	—
Tsuga canadensis	540	21,800	1.6	—	—
HARDWOODS					
Acer saccharum	530	18,060	6.3	—	—
Acer sp.	550	—	—	—	12–14
Alnus rubra	—	19,600	6.0	—	—
Betula alleghaniensis	530	22,250	1.7	—	—
Betula sp.	490	—	—	71–79	13–17
Fagus sylvatica	710	16,560	7.2	68–82	6–8
Platanus occidentalis	—	18,400	5.8	—	—
Populus tremula	400	—	—	95–106	13–15
Populus tremuloides	450	20,750	4.0	—	—
Quercus alba	—	17,400	10.7	—	—
Quercus sp.	—	17,140	6.8	—	17–22
Salix nigra	—	17,900	6.0	—	—
Ulmus americana	250	17,250	9.5	—	—

*After Fournier and Goulet (1970) and other sources. Key: —, data not available.

Photographs of Bark Structure

The structures of the bast and of the rhytidome described in this chapter are illustrated by a dozen macrophotographs followed by the same number of photomicrographs. This special grouping has been set apart in order to make reading the main text easier. The macrophotographs (the photographs with the scale bars) show the most important characters in transverse (cross) section. Most of these same characters are shown in the photomicrographs (taken through a microscope), which follow. The captions present simplified descriptions, and for simplicity, we have not presented radial or tangential sections.

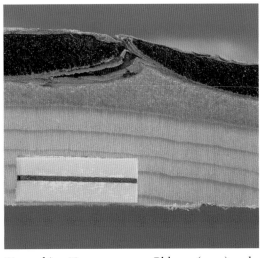

Picea abies, Norway spruce. Phloem (gray) and rhytidome scales (brown). Scale bar, 1 cm.

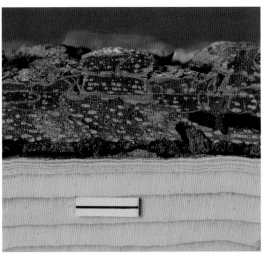

Picea abies, Norway spruce. Clumps of stone cells (light spots) in the rhytidome of an old tree. Scale bar, 1 cm.

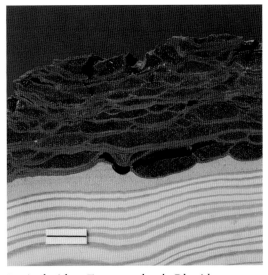

Larix decidua, European larch. Rhytidome scales. Scale bar, 1 cm.

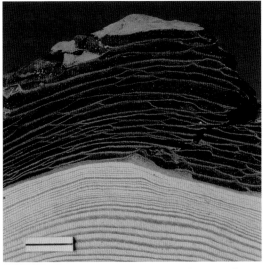

Pinus sylvestris, Scots pine. Rhytidome scales. Scale bar, 1 cm.

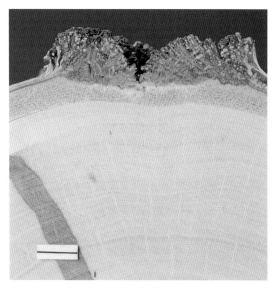

Betula sp., birch. Lenticel. Scale bar, 1 cm.

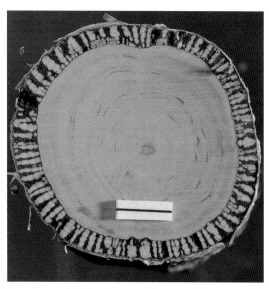

Betula sp., birch. Clumps of stony cells oriented radially (light spots). Scale bar, 1 cm.

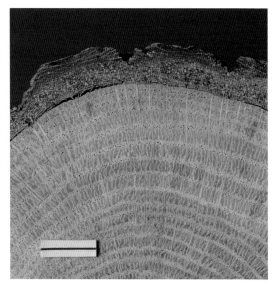

Quercus sp., oak. Phloem fibers (tangential bands) and stone cells (light spots). Scale bar, 1 cm.

Robinia pseudoacacia, black locust. Structures resembling annual rings characterized by phloem fibers (pale bands). Scale bar, 1 cm.

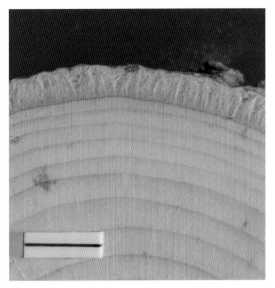

Tilia sp., linden. Dilatation of phloem rays (funnel-shaped pale zones) cutting at first through the smooth bark. Scale bar, 1 cm.

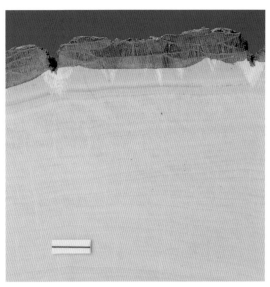

Tilia sp., linden. Formation of rhytidome in an old tree. Dilatation of the phloem rays, particularly beneath the grooves between the rhytidome scales. Scale bar, 1 cm.

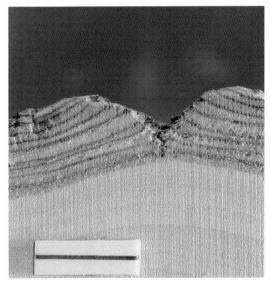

Sambucus nigra, black elderberry. Structures resembling annual rings characterized by the distribution of cell contents. Scale bar, 1 cm.

Clematis vitalba, traveler's joy. Annular rhytidome. Scale bar, 1 cm.

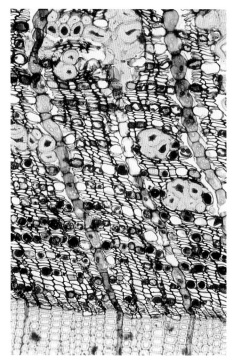

Abies alba, European silver fir. Clumps of stone cells (yellow). Transverse section, ×110.

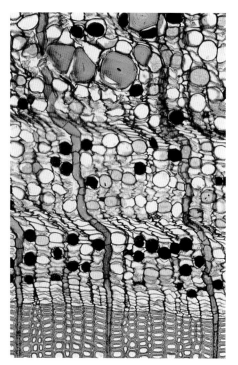

Larix decidua, European larch. Isolated stone cells (yellow). Transverse section, ×110.

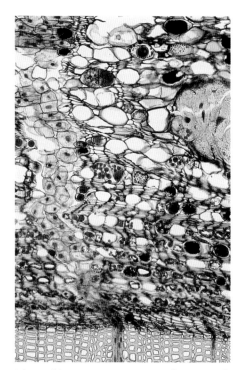

Picea abies, Norway spruce. Dilatation of the phloem rays (purple) and a clump of stone cells (yellow). Transverse section, ×110.

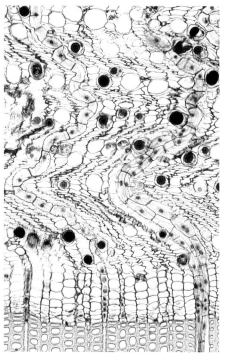

Pinus sylvestris, Scots pine. Severe cellular collapse and wavy lines of phloem rays. Transverse section, ×110.

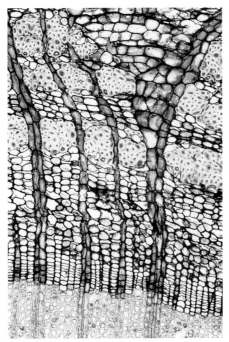

Fraxinus excelsior, European ash. Phloem fibers arranged in bands and dilatation of the phloem rays (funnel). Transverse section, ×110.

Acer sp., maple. Phloem fibers (white) and clumps of stone cells (yellow). Transverse section, ×110.

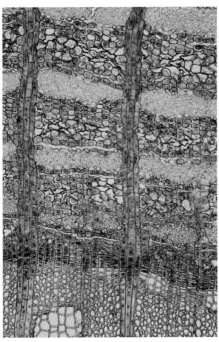

Robinia pseudoacacia, black locust. The bands of phloem fibers (white) are cut by the radial lines of the phloem rays (purple). Transverse section, ×110.

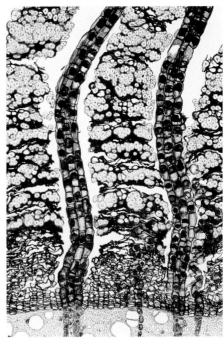

Prunus avium, mazzard cherry. Splits between the broad phloem rays (purple) and the rest of the tissue created by collapse of the sieve tubes. Transverse section, ×110.

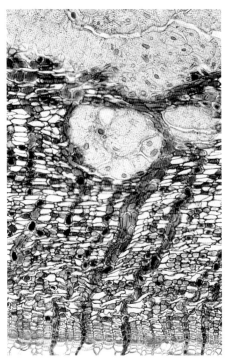

Betula sp., birch. Large mass of stone cells (white). Transverse section, ×110.

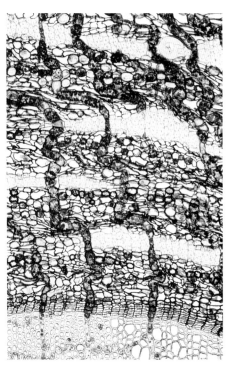

Quercus sp., oak. Bands of phloem fibers (white) cut by wavy lines of phloem rays. Transverse section, ×110.

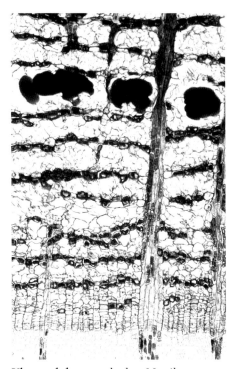

Ulmus glabra, wych elm. Mucilage-containing cavities (deep blue). Transverse section, ×110.

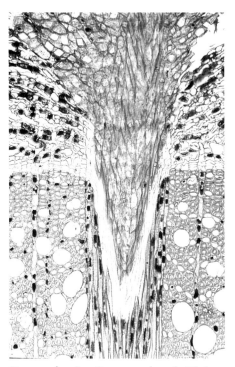

Fagus sylvatica, European beech. Wedge-shaped growth and dilatation of the phloem rays, with deposits of crystals (blue-black). Transverse section, ×110.

CHAPTER 3
THE ETHNOBOTANY OF BARK

N EUROPE, including Russia, the total quantity of wood harvested in 1987 reached nearly 750 million cubic meters (nearly a billion cubic yards). If the bark represents between 5 and 10% of the volume of wood, and taking an average of 7%, that makes the volume of bark more than 50 million cubic meters (65 million cubic yards), which would fill a freight train 10,000 km (6200 miles) long! Only a tiny fraction of this material is recovered industrially. The economic need for raw materials and for energy should encourage those responsible for the wood pipeline to give bark a higher value. Research in progress to improve procedures for the industrial exploitation of bark will probably open up new possibilities that take advantage of its special qualities.

ENERGY SOURCE

Some furnaces specially designed for the burning of cork feed into central heating systems or into electrical generators. Nonetheless, the burning of bark to generate energy poses difficulties resulting from problems of transport, storage, presence of potentially polluting chemicals, and water content (Deschênes, 1986, p. 109). On a small scale, briquettes for home heating are made with pellets of bark.

AGRICULTURE, HORTICULTURE, AND ANIMAL HUSBANDRY

Since the 1960s in the United States and the 1980s in Europe, various grades of shredded bark products have been added to soils that are poor in humus. Shredded or ground bark has also been used as an amendment for soils with weak structure, as a substitute for peat, or as a decorative ground cover. This organic matter has applications in the growing of soft fruits, the transplanting of trees, and in kitchen gardens, terrace gardens, and soilless cultivation systems.

Pulverized bark has also been made into bedding for domesticated animals. Horticulturally or arboriculturally, it can be used as a mulch and to maintain humidity for plants that are sensitive to excessive sunlight.

ABSORPTION AND FILTERING

The ability of finely pulverized dry bark to absorb fluids is very good, even better than that of wood sawdust. It has been used successfully to absorb water, and oil and oil residues, not only from soil, but also from water.

In addition to absorbing the odor of manure in animal pens, bark can be used to filter out the odors from biological toilets and other sources of foul-smelling gases. The activity of bark as a biofilter in treating gases is because of the microorganisms that it contains (Deschênes, 1986, p. 111).

CONSTRUCTION MATERIAL

Some public parks, sports facilities, and botanical gardens have pathways made from uniformly sized chips of bark and wood. Running tracks and horse racing tracks have also been constructed from this relatively cheap material.

FIBER

A number of studies have been published on the fabrication of particle boards, fiber boards, and insulating and decorative panels using crushed or ground bark as a substitute for wood sawdust. For certain ordinary grades of paper, corrugated and regular cardboard, and roofing shingles, a small percentage of bark pulp can be added during manufacture, but the slurry obtained in this way is of lower quality than that made from wood pulp alone, without added bark.

The bark of certain trees is referred to as bast or bass, a bark in which the inner living part, the secondary phloem, is rich in long, tough, durable fibers. This is the case with elm (*Ulmus*), black locust (*Robinia pseudoacacia*), and linden (*Tilia*), especially little-leaf linden (*T. cordata*), in which the bark, after appropriate treatment, releases textile fibers that are used by basket weavers to make ropes, mats, and other coarse but flexible objects.

In the region of Vancouver, Canada, aboriginal people traditionally made waterproof cloaks, mats, sails, and ropes with the bast from incense cedar (*Calocedrus decurrens*). They have also used it to cover the roofs of their houses. In the countries of northern Europe, the bark of birch (*Betula*), which is highly resistant to decay, also serves to cover some house roofs as well as being used for making mats, ropes, baskets, and household items.

There was a time when writing paper was made from thin layers of the peeled bark of paper birch (*Betula papyrifera*) and heath-leaf paperbark (*Melaleuca styphelioides*). The bark of young shoots of paper mulberry (*Broussonetia papyrifera*), after a long maceration in alkaline water, is used to make the famous satiny, pearly mulberry paper of China and Japan.

CORK

Cork oak (*Quercus suber*) is virtually without parallel among trees. It is the only one that is exploited industrially and exclusively for its bark: cork, a raw material whose properties are nearly impossible to duplicate artificially. This tree of the Mediterranean countries and of the adjacent Atlantic coasts is cultivated principally in Portugal, which with 150–200 million kilograms (330–440 million pounds) per year provides 50% of world production. Portugal has more than 750 thousand hectares (1.8 million acres) of cork oaks under cultivation. Next come Spain, Algeria, Morocco, France, Italy, and Tunisia.

A standardized procedure is used for harvesting cork. When the cork oak reaches the age of 20–25 years and its trunk measures about 30 cm (12 inches) in diameter, it can be debarked (or stripped) for the first time. The virgin cork from this harvest is of low quality and is generally only used for granulated cork. After another 8–10 years, the cork will have regrown to a thickness of 3–5 cm (1¼–2 inches). The second harvest can then proceed, and thenceforth every 8–10 years to an age of 130–150 years if the tree holds up well and grows in favorable climatic conditions. Trees that are not subjected to this harvesting regime can live 300–400 years!

The uniqueness of the cork oak lies in the great ease with which the outer bark (cork and rhytidome) can be separated from the inner bark (bast), preserving the living part that produces the cork. The art of stripping, which is carried out from mid-June to mid-August (while the sap is rising), lies in making longitudinal and then horizontal cuts on the trunk in order to release strips or sheets without damaging the inner bark. Thus the growth of cork can resume without initiating faults in the new cork. The living bark, which is reddish yellow after debarking, gradually turns ochre thereafter, then brownish red over the course of weeks, and finally blackish gray after about a year.

Although cork is a dead bark, it should be considered a noble plant material since its intrinsic properties are numerous and irreplaceable by any single synthetic material of the same cost. The qualities of cork can be summarized as follows: lightness (density of 0.15–0.25 g/cm^3), good resistance to compression and bending, good elasticity, great capacity to absorb vibration, very high coefficient of friction, low coefficient of swelling, very low heat conduction, inertness to chemical agents and to boiling in water (100°C, 212°F), very good resistance to absorption, impermeability to moisture, excellent durability and freedom from decay, nearly noninflammable, good coefficient of noise absorption, and handsome appearance, permitting its use for decorative articles.

The industrial and small-scale applications of cork are as varied as they are numerous. Its most familiar use is as stoppers (corks) for bottles of wine, champagne, whiskey, etc. However, the largest volume of cork consumed by industry actually goes into the manufacture of cork aggregate soundproofing panels and cork tiles used as flooring in private homes, public buildings, factories, sports halls, etc. Significant quantities of cork are also used to make sheets of various thickness that are used in light carpentry and for interior decoration.

The list of products that are made wholly or partly of cork is impressive. We can cite, in no particular order: floats for fishnets; life preservers; antivibration blocks for machinery; insulation for appliances, including refrigerators; watertight couplings and washers; standardized sheets of different thickness (just like paper); cigarette filters; vapor barriers; parts for toys; linings for carrying cases; blocks for printing on bags, fabrics, or wallpaper; tabletops, trays, and cork boards; model making by sculptors and architects; boxes and decorative objects sculpted from cork; insulating covers; polishing wheels for the glass industry; articles for sports, education, and handicrafts; shipping cases and protective packing material for fragile commodities; packing material for pharmaceutical products; parts for footwear, clogs, and orthopedic devices; etc. One could also mention the aerospace industry, which uses cork for its qualities of lightness coupled with good thermal insulation. The books by Cook (1961), Dessain and Tondelier (1991), and Oliveira and Oliveira (1991) have more information on cork and the cork oak.

Bark may contain a wide variety of chemical constituents such as tannins, waxes, essential oils, resins, gums, mucilages, and latices, and a variety of binders, glues, adhesives, drugs, and spices may be obtained by crushing and distilling various barks. Some specific examples are cited in the remaining sections of this chapter.

TANNINS AND DYES

Tannins are substances that may be found in many plant organs, including the barks of oak (*Quercus*), alder (*Alnus*), birch (*Betula*), etc. They render animal skins resistant to decay, which is why tannins are used in making leather. Tannins also furnish inks of different colors. In medicine, they are used in astringent tonics. Since about 1960, natural plant-derived tannins have been rivaled by synthetic products.

Tan (or tanbark) is the bark of oak or chestnut (*Aesculus*) that has been reduced to a reddish brown powder. Of all the European oaks, kermes oak (*Quercus coccifera*) is richest in tannin, with 11–16%. However, the most prized tannin comes from holm oak (*Q. ilex*). The tannin obtained from European alder (*Alnus glutinosa*) is gray. It is used in northern countries to tan hides. The bark of Norway spruce (*Picea abies*) also contains a tannin, as do the barks of certain pines. That of Aleppo pine (*Pinus halepensis*) is 13–15% tannin. Reduced to powder, it was formerly mixed with the tanbark of kermes oak. The tannin of tamarisk (*Tamarix*), from the bark and leafy twigs, was also used for tanning skins and as a dye. There are numerous species of trees containing tannins that are used as dyes. In southern Chile, there has been a report of the value of three ancient practices in the making of woven cloth on primitive looms using handmade wool and dyes based on bark sawdust in the following shades: beige-green, greenish yellow, coffee brown, and reddish copper. The following examples indicate the range of colors that may be obtained from bark dyes:

Aesculus hippocastanum, horse chestnut	red
Amelanchier ovalis, snowy mespil	slightly golden pale beige
Cotinus coggygria, smoke tree	yellow-orange
Juglans regia, Persian walnut	golden brown or coffee brown
Ligustrum vulgare, privet	yellow
Populus nigra, black poplar	golden yellow
Prunus spinosa, sloe	black in the presence of iron sulfate
Quercus velutina, eastern black oak	bright yellow or lemon
Rhamnus saxatilis subsp. *tinctorius,* dyer's buckthorn	yellow
Rhus coriaria, tanner's sumac	red or yellow

SPICES AND INCENSE

The barks of certain trees are exploited as spices and sometimes for their fragrance. Cascarilla bark (*Croton eluteria*) tablets and incense sticks emit a pleasant scent and are prepared from the bark. Cinnamon (*Cinnamomum verum*) in the form of dry bark or powder is a spice used in confectioneries and in various liqueurs. It is obtained by separating the bark and bast from young shoots of the cinnamon tree. Winter bark (*Drimys winteri*) is reduced to a powder. It has a strong odor, resembling that of cinnamon, and is used for flavoring certain foods. Sandalwood (*Santalum album*) is prized for its fragrant wood; the bark and sticks of sandalwood are burned as incense.

Bark in Phytotherapy, by Beat Meier

In comparison to leaves, roots, and medicinal herbs, barks play a subsidiary role in phytotherapy, that is, therapy using phytomedicines, which may be defined as medicines containing only plants, parts of plants, or plant materials, or combinations thereof, as active ingredients, whether in crude form or processed. For example, in the second edition of the book *Teedrogen* (herbal drugs), edited by M. Wichtl (Stuttgart, 1989), a compendium of medicinal plants in use in Germany, there are only 11 articles referring to bark out of a total of 241. This may result in part from the fact that the number of plants producing usable bark is relatively limited. Phytotherapy attempts to explain the efficacy of medicinal plants by the presence of products of secondary metabolism. The secondary tissues of the bark are not directly connected to the pool of secondary metabolites. In effect, barks with a well-developed rhytidome are generally low in cellular contents. The instructions for gathering bark for "salicis cortex" and "quercus cortex" are typical. It is recommended that bark be collected from 2- to 3-year-old shoots or from young stump sprouts rather than from larger trunks with thicker, more mature bark. The bark for "cinnamomi cortex," obtained from young suckers growing out from cut stumps, lacks outer bark and comes away free from the cambial layer beneath.

Although the number of barks used in phytotherapy is small, their place in the history of the discovery of medicines is disproportionately significant. Certain important active substances (including quinine, quinidine, and salicin) have been isolated from bark and introduced into therapy just as they are or in a modified form.

Salicin, a substance found in the leaves as well as in the bark of willows and poplars, plants of the family Salicaceae (*Salix* and *Populus*), stimulated the development of acetylsalicylic acid (aspirin), used in enormous quantities as a painkiller since 1899. Attempts were made to use salicin as an analgesic in the first half of the 19th century, using an active substance extracted from the bark of willow. As we now know, the esters of salicin contained in the Salicaceae (such as salicortin, tremulacin, and 2′-*O*-aceytylsalicortin) become hydrolyzed, shortening their useful life in therapy. As a result, it was easier to produce synthetic salicylic acid and acetylsalicylic acid than to make stable preparations from the bark. Salicin and acetylsalicylic acid are hardly distinguishable in their analgesic and antipyretic effects. It has been shown that the array of metabolites of salicin corresponds to that of acetylsalicylic acid, that salicin is absorbed from a bark extract, and that its presence in the blood can be confirmed, like that of salicylic acid. That is why one might also expect an effect for the natural extract. Because of this, dry extracts of willow bark adjusted to a titer of 60–120 mg of salicin daily have resumed their importance in phytotherapy as a remedy for headaches and rheumatism. Salicin has the advantage of lacking the unstable acetyl group of acetylsalicylic acid, which has been shown to reduce the clotting ability of blood platelets through the inhibition of cyclo-oxygenases. It has the further advantage that the acid group, which attacks mucous membranes, is present in a reduced form in the molecule. Research has made it possible to define more precisely the range of potential source plants. All species of willow investigated have been shown to produce esters of salicin in sufficient quantity for phytotherapeutic use. Willows and poplars are counted among the medicinal plants with gentle effects.

Dry willow bark can be used to prepare a bitter tea that reinforces antirheumatic therapies. Nevertheless, given the diversity of the species, there is a risk of using a bark that contains little or no salicin, so it is better to rely on a manufactured and standardized product for treatment.

The bark of the quinine tree (*Cinchona pubescens*), "cinchonae cortex," was first used as a febrifuge and only later in the treatment of malaria. This use is largely superseded today by synthetic medicines that are more effective and have fewer side effects. The bark of the quinine tree contains large quantities of alkaloids (5–15%) among which quinine and quinidine have made their way into therapy. Physicians specializing in tropical diseases use quinine more frequently than they have for the specific case of a strain of *Plasmodium falciparum* that is becoming resistant to other drugs. The substance also retains its importance as a bitter drug. Quinine is among the most bitter substances known, so much so that the quantities imparting a strong flavor to tonic waters for drinking are pharmacologically inactive. The phytotherapeutic dose, however, is effective at the same low levels. Quinine bark extract of a measured dose is used in stomachics and roborants (strengthening drugs), which stimulate the appetite and gastric juices. It is also used as a fortifier along with vitamins, mineral salts, and other bitter drugs, for example "condurango cortex" (*Gonolobus cundurango*), which contains bitter substances resembling saponins. The action of the quinidine stereoisomer is completely different. It is only synthesized in tiny quantities in the plant and does not, therefore, have any significance in phytotherapy. Physicians use quinidine specifically for treating certain forms of cardiac arrhythmia. As an alkaloid-containing drug, quinine bark counts among the strong medicinal plants, so much so that it should only be used as a roborant in a carefully measured dose.

The group of drugs containing anthraquinones also belongs among the medicinal plants with strong actions. Conditioned by the physiological transformation of the inactive plant protodrug into active substances, the laxative effect of anthraquinones only makes itself felt after 6–8 hours. The anthraquinones irritate only the large intestine, as desired, and not the stomach. "Frangula cortex" (*Rhamnus frangula*) and "rhamnus purshiani cortex" (*R. purshiana*) should be stored warm and dry for a year or more before being used because it takes time for the anthrone in the fresh drug to be transformed into anthraquinone. These two barks hold a special place compared to the other drugs containing anthracene ("aloe," "rhei radix," "sennae fructus," and "sennae folium") because they have fewer undesirable side effects. The problem with continuous use of natural laxatives is that heightened irritation of the large intestine provokes an artificial state of persistent intestinal inactivity that can cause the drugs to lose their effectiveness. For this reason anthraquinone therapy is only practical in the short term and when it is absolutely necessary, for example, while traveling. The correct and occasional use of laxatives is harmless. If diarrhea occurs, however, it is essential to reduce the dose as treatment continues, leading to soft and pliant stools. The optimal dose is that which is just effective. It is difficult to dose herbal teas appropriately, so one should take only controlled preparations.

Phytomedicines may be divided into the categories of "forte" and "mite." The latter tend to be more gentle in their action and consequently tend to have a broader range of dosage phytotherapeutically. However, they sometimes have limits to their use, for example, in the case of diagnosed ailments. The bark of cinnamon (*Cinnamomum verum*), "cinnamomi cortex," can be used without hesitation in the realm of foodstuffs or in phytotherapy, given that the powder is used more often as a spice than as a remedy. As a remedy, it has the following effects: stomachic, digestive, and carminative in cases of flatulence, dyspepsia, and lack of appetite. The best form is a tincture in which the odor and flavor develop. The use of the essential oil (constituting at least 1.2% of the bark) in popular medicine for treatment of dysmenorrhea has become more attractive since it has been shown that the biosynthesis of prostaglandins can be impeded through the inhibition of cyclo-oxygenase, a process that has been demonstrated in vitro.

"Quercus cortex" (*Quercus robur* and *Q. petraea*) is one of the most important tannin-containing phytomedicines. Its use is topical, in the form of a rinse or gargle, either of which can be prepared by adding add two spoonfuls of bark cut from young shoots to 500 ml (about a pint) of water. To prepare a bath, boil 500 g (about a pound) of oak bark in 4–5 liters (about 4–5 quarts) of water about 15–20 minutes, then pour this solution into the bathwater. The standard formulary of the public health office of Germany lists the following applications: relief for irritation of the gums and of the mucous membranes of the mouth, reduction of excessive sweating of the feet, and treatment of chilblains and anal fissures. "Hamamelidis cortex" (*Hamamelis virginiana*) is similar except that in addition to topical use as a gargle, it can be swallowed to enhance the treatment of nonspecific acute diarrhea. The bark as well as the leaves are extracted and employed in different remedies for skin diseases, wounds, hemorrhoids, and diseases of the veins.

These examples of barks used in phytotherapy provide far from a complete accounting, there being many other applications in popular medicine. The rediscovery of the Celtic tree almanac and careful study of the mythology of trees has enabled us to rediscover old knowledge of the medicinal virtues of bark and to understand them through phytopharmacological research.

One of the most recently discovered medicinal uses of bark is in the treatment of ovarian cancer. Paclitaxel, commonly called taxol, is found throughout the tissues of the leaves and stems of all species of yew trees (*Taxus*) and in some of their close relatives. It is even produced by cells of yews grown in tissue culture or suspension culture. In the United States, however, the sole approved pharmaceutical source is by extraction from the bark of Pacific yew (*T. brevifolia*). Since this species is not cultivated for this purpose and harvesting the bark kills the tree, Pacific yew is becoming scarce in the forests of the Pacific Northwest. Paclitaxel is a very powerful and toxic drug and should never be taken without medical supervision. (This paragraph is added by the translator.)

CHAPTER 4
THE
BARKS

Abies alba, European silver fir, Pinaceae; southern Europe, photographed in the Swiss Jura.

Abies cephalonica, Grecian fir, Pinaceae; southern Europe, photographed in Montriant Park, Geneva, Switzerland.

Abies cilicica, Cilician fir, Pinaceae; western Asia, photographed in the Thuret Garden, Cap d'Antibes, France.

Abies concolor, white fir, Pinaceae; western North America, photographed in the Geneva Botanical Garden, Switzerland.

Abies firma, momi fir, Pinaceae; eastern Asia, photographed on Mainau Island, Lake Constance, Germany.

Abies grandis, grand fir, Pinaceae; eastern North America, photographed in the Forest Trial Garden, Grafrath, Germany.

Abies homolepis, Nikko fir, Pinaceae; eastern Asia, photographed in the Royal Botanic Gardens, Kew, England.

Abies lasiocarpa, subalpine fir, Pinaceae; western North America, photographed in the Rocky Mountains, British Columbia, Canada.

Abies nordmanniana, Caucasian fir, Pinaceae; western Asia, photographed at Fota House, Ireland.

Abies nordmanniana, Caucasian fir, Pinaceae; western Asia, photographed on Mainau Island, Lake Constance, Germany.

Abies pinsapo, Spanish fir, Pinaceae; southern Europe, photographed in a park in Geneva, Switzerland.

Abies procera, noble fir, Pinaceae; western North America, photographed in the Forest Trial Garden, Grafrath, Germany.

Abies sibirica, Siberian balsam fir, Pinaceae; northern Asia, photographed in the Forest Trial Garden, Grafrath, Germany.

Abies squamata, flaky fir, Pinaceae; eastern Asia, photographed in the Hillier Arboretum, England.

Abies veitchii, Veitch fir, Pinaceae; eastern Asia, photographed in the Forest Trial Garden, Grafrath, Germany.

Acer buergerianum, trident maple, Sapindaceae; eastern Asia, photographed in the Strybing Arboretum, San Francisco, California. *Acer* continued p. 58.

Acacia dealbata, silver wattle, Leguminosae; Australia,
photographed on Isola Madre, Lake Maggiore, Italy.

Acer campestre, field maple, Sapindaceae; Europe, photographed in the Swiss Jura.

Acer campestre, field maple, Sapindaceae; Europe, photographed in the vicinity of Bienne, Switzerland.

Acer capillipes, red snakebark maple, Sapindaceae; eastern Asia, photographed at Maplewood Nursery, Roseburg, Oregon.

Acer cissifolium, ivy-leaf maple, Sapindaceae; eastern Asia, photographed at Mount Congreve, Ireland.

Acer davidii, snakebark maple, Sapindaceae; eastern Asia,
photographed in the Royal Botanic Gardens, Kew, England.

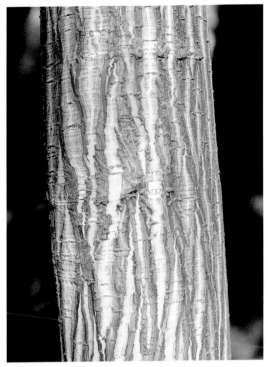

Acer davidii, snakebark maple, Sapindaceae; eastern Asia, photographed in the University of British Columbia Botanical Garden, Vancouver, Canada.

Acer davidii, snakebark maple, Sapindaceae; eastern Asia, photographed in the Royal Botanic Gardens, Kew, England.

Acer davidii subsp. *grosseri*, snakebark maple, Sapindaceae; eastern Asia, photographed in the Strybing Arboretum, San Francisco, California.

Acer davidii 'Hersii', snakebark maple, Sapindaceae; eastern Asia, photographed in the Arboretum des Barres, Nogent-sur-Vernisson, France.

Acer griseum, paperbark maple, Sapindaceae; eastern Asia,
photographed in the Royal Botanic Gardens, Kew, England.

Acer griseum, paperbark maple, Sapindaceae; eastern Asia, photographed in the Royal Botanic Gardens, Kew, England.

Acer griseum, paperbark maple, Sapindaceae; eastern Asia,
photographed in the Royal Botanic Gardens, Kew, England.

Acer griseum, paperbark maple, Sapindaceae; eastern Asia, photographed in the Royal Botanic Gardens, Kew, England.

Acer heldreichii subsp. *trautvetteri*, redbud maple, Sapindaceae; western Asia, photographed on Mainau Island, Lake Constance, Germany.

Acer macrophyllum, big-leaf maple, Sapindaceae; western North America, photographed in the Washington Park Arboretum, Seattle, Washington.

Acer maximowiczianum, Nikko maple, Sapindaceae; eastern Asia, photographed in the Van Gimborn Arboretum, Netherlands.

Acer macrophyllum, big-leaf maple, Sapindaceae; western North America, photographed in the Washington Park Arboretum, Seattle, Washington.

Acer miyabei, Miyabe maple, Sapindaceae; eastern Asia, photographed in the University of British Columbia Botanical Garden, Vancouver, Canada.

Acer mono, painted maple, Sapindaceae; eastern Asia, photographed in the Royal Botanic Gardens, Kew, England.

Acer monspessulanum, Montpellier maple, Sapindaceae; southern Europe, photographed in a park in Geneva, Switzerland.

Acer negundo, box elder, Sapindaceae; North America, photographed in the Padua Botanical Garden, Italy.

Acer opalus, Italian maple, Sapindaceae; southern Europe, photographed in the Arboretum des Barres, Nogent-sur-Vernisson, France.

Acer pensylvanicum, moosewood, Sapindaceae; eastern North America, photographed in the Trompenburg Arboretum, Netherlands.

Acer pensylvanicum 'Erythrocladum', moosewood, Sapindaceae; eastern North America, photographed in the Hillier Arboretum, England.

Acer pentaphyllum, five-leaf maple, Sapindaceae; eastern Asia, photographed in the Strybing Arboretum, San Francisco, California.

Acer platanoides, Norway maple, Sapindaceae; Europe, photographed on the Swiss Plateau.

Acer pseudoplatanus, sycamore maple, Sapindaceae; Europe, photographed in the Swiss Jura.

Acer pseudoplatanus, sycamore maple, Sapindaceae; Europe, photographed in the vicinity of Bienne, Switzerland.

Acer rufinerve, red-vein maple, Sapindaceae; eastern Asia, photographed in the Royal Botanic Gardens, Kew, England.

Acer rubrum, red maple, Sapindaceae; eastern North America,
photographed in the Geneva Botanical Garden, Switzerland.

Acer saccharinum 'Wieri Laciniatum', silver maple, Sapindaceae; eastern North America, photographed in the Royal Botanic Gardens, Kew, England.

Acer saccharum subsp. *leucoderme*, chalk maple, Sapindaceae; eastern North America, photographed in the Geneva Botanical Garden, Switzerland.

Acer tegmentosum, Manchurian stripe-bark maple, Sapindaceae; eastern Asia, photographed in the Zürich Botanical Garden, Switzerland.

Acer ×zoeschense, maple, Sapindaceae; southern Europe, photographed in the Royal Botanic Gardens, Kew, England.

Adansonia digitata, baobab, Malvaceae; tropical Africa, photographed at Venda, South Africa.

Adansonia digitata, baobab, Malvaceae; tropical Africa, photographed in the Nelspruit Botanical Garden, South Africa.

Aesculus assamica, Assam horse chestnut, Sapindaceae; southern Asia, photographed in the Royal Botanic Gardens, Kew, England.

Aesculus ×bushii, horse chestnut, Sapindaceae; eastern North America, photographed in the Royal Botanic Gardens, Kew, England.

Aesculus ×carnea, red horse chestnut, Sapindaceae; originated in cultivation, photographed in the Vallon d'Aubonne Arboretum, Vaud, Switzerland.

Aesculus hippocastanum, horse chestnut, Sapindaceae; eastern Europe, photographed in the vicinity of Bienne, Switzerland.

Aesculus hippocastanum, horse chestnut, Sapindaceae; eastern Europe, photographed in the vicinity of Bienne, Switzerland.

Aesculus turbinata, Japanese horse chestnut, Sapindaceae; eastern Asia, photographed in the Vallon d'Aubonne Arboretum, Vaud, Switzerland.

Agathis robusta, Queensland kauri pine, Araucariaceae; northeastern Australia, photographed in the Pamplemousses Botanical Garden, Mauritius.

Agathis robusta, Queensland kauri pine, Araucariaceae; northeastern Australia, photographed in the Pamplemousses Botanical Garden, Mauritius.

Ailanthus altissima, tree of heaven, Simaroubaceae; eastern Asia,
photographed in the Lausanne Botanical Garden, Switzerland.

Ailanthus altissima, tree of heaven, Simaroubaceae; eastern Asia, photographed in the Vallon
d'Aubonne Arboretum, Vaud, Switzerland.

Albizia saman, rain tree, Leguminosae; tropical
America, photographed in the Orotava Acclimatization Garden, Tenerife, Spain.

Alluaudia sp., Didiereaceae; Madagascar, photographed in South Africa.

Alnus glutinosa, European alder, Betulaceae;
Europe, photographed on the Swiss Plateau.

Alnus glutinosa, European alder, Betulaceae;
Europe, photographed in the Royal Botanic
Gardens, Kew, England.

Alnus incana, gray alder, Betulaceae; northern
Eurasia, photographed in the Swiss Alps.

Alnus incana, gray alder, Betulaceae; northern
Eurasia, photographed in the Royal Botanic
Gardens, Kew, England.

Alnus rubra, red alder, Betulaceae; western
North America, photographed in the Royal
Botanic Gardens, Kew, England.

Angophora costata, smooth-barked Australian apple, Myrtaceae; eastern Australia, photographed in the Thuret Garden, Cap d'Antibes, France.

Antidesma venosum, tassel berry, Euphorbiaceae; southern Africa, photographed in the Nelspruit Botanical Garden, South Africa.

Araucaria araucana, monkey-puzzle tree, Araucariaceae; southern South America, photographed in Montriant Park, Geneva, Switzerland.

Araucaria araucana, monkey-puzzle tree, Araucariaceae; southern South America, photographed at Kilmacurragh, Ireland.

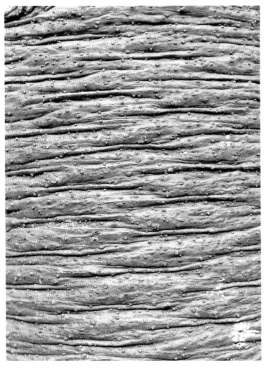

Araucaria araucana, monkey-puzzle tree, Araucariaceae; southern South America, photographed in the Royal Botanic Gardens, Kew, England.

Araucaria bidwillii, bunya pine, Araucariaceae; eastern Australia, photographed in the Thuret Garden, Cap d'Antibes, France.

Araucaria columnaris, New Caledonian pine or Cook's pine, Araucariaceae; New Caledonia, photographed in the Pamplemousses Botanical Garden, Mauritius.

Araucaria cunninghamii, hoop pine, Araucariaceae; eastern Australia, photographed in the Hanbury Garden, La Mortola, Italy.

Arbutus ×andrachnoides, hybrid strawberry tree, Ericaceae; southern
Europe, photographed in the Dublin Botanical Garden, Ireland.

Arbutus canariensis, Canary Island strawberry tree, Ericaceae; Canary Islands, photographed in the Strybing Arboretum, San Francisco, California.

Arbutus menziesii, Pacific madrone, Ericaceae; western North America, photographed in a national forest in Oregon.

Arbutus unedo, strawberry tree, Ericaceae; southern Europe, photographed in the Thuret Garden, Cap d'Antibes, France.

Arctostaphylos manzanita, Parry manzanita, Ericaceae; western North America, photographed in Van Damme (Pygmy Forest) State Park, California.

Bactris cf. *gasipaes,* peach palm, Palmae; Central America, photographed in the Pamplemousses Botanical Garden, Mauritius.

Arctostaphylos glandulosa, Eastwood manzanita, Ericaceae; southwestern
North America, photographed in the Thuret Garden, Cap d'Antibes, France.

Betula albo-sinensis, Chinese red birch, Betulaceae; eastern Asia, photographed at Malahide Castle, Ireland.

Betula albo-sinensis var. **septentrionalis,** northern Chinese red birch, Betulaceae; eastern Asia, photographed in the Vallon d'Aubonne Arboretum, Vaud, Switzerland.

Betula alleghaniensis, yellow birch, Betulaceae; eastern North America, photographed in the Royal Botanic Gardens, Kew, England.

Betula alnoides, alder birch, Betulaceae; Himalaya, photographed in the Royal Botanic Gardens, Kew, England.

Betula costata, Korean gray birch, Betulaceae; eastern Asia, photographed on the island of Ilnacullin (Garnish Island), Ireland.

Betula davurica, Mongolian black birch, Betulaceae; eastern Asia, photographed in the Padua Botanical Garden, Italy.

Betula ermanii, Erman's birch, Betulaceae; eastern Asia, photographed at Birr Castle, Ireland.

Betula lenta, sweet birch, Betulaceae; eastern North America, photographed in the Forest Trial Garden, Grafrath, Germany.

Betula maximowicziana, monarch birch, Betulaceae; eastern Asia, photographed in the Vallon d'Aubonne Arboretum, Vaud, Switzerland.

Betula nigra, river birch, Betulaceae; eastern North America, photographed in the Vallon d'Aubonne Arboretum, Vaud, Switzerland.

Betula nigra, river birch, Betulaceae; eastern North America, photographed in the Zürich Botanical Garden, Switzerland.

Betula papyrifera, paper birch, Betulaceae; northern North America, photographed in the Vallon d'Aubonne Arboretum, Vaud, Switzerland.

Betula pendula, European white birch, Betulaceae; northern Europe, photographed in a cemetery in St. Gall, Switzerland.

Betula pendula, European white birch, Betulaceae; northern Europe, photographed in the vicinity of Bienne, Switzerland.

Betula platyphylla, Manchurian white birch, Betulaceae; eastern Asia, photographed in the Vallon d'Aubonne Arboretum, Vaud, Switzerland.

Betula platyphylla var. *japonica,* Japanese white birch, Betulaceae; eastern Asia, photographed in the Royal Botanic Gardens, Kew, England.

Betula pubescens, downy white birch, Betulaceae; northern Europe, photographed in the Zürich Botanical Garden, Switzerland.

Betula ×sandbergii, hybrid bog birch, Betulaceae; eastern North America, photographed in the Royal Botanic Gardens, Kew, England.

Betula utilis var. *jacquemontii*, Himalayan red birch, Betulaceae; Himalaya, photographed in the Royal Botanic Gardens, Kew, England.

Brachychiton discolor, Queensland lacebark, Malvaceae; northeastern Australia, photographed in the Orotava Acclimatization Garden, Tenerife, Spain.

Betula utilis var. *jacquemontii,* Himalayan red birch, Betulaceae; Himalaya,
photographed in the Vallon d'Aubonne Arboretum, Vaud, Switzerland.

Brachychiton populneus, kurrajong, Malvaceae; eastern Australia, photographed in the Thuret Garden, Cap d'Antibes, France.

Brahea armata, Mexican blue fan palm, Palmae; northwestern Mexico, photographed on the Côte d'Azur, France.

Brochoneura acuminata, Madagascar bleeding nutmeg, Myristicaceae; Madagascar, photographed in the Pamplemousses Botanical Garden, Mauritius.

Broussonetia papyrifera, paper mulberry, Moraceae; eastern Asia, photographed in the St. Gall Botanical Garden, Switzerland.

Bursera simaruba, gumbo limbo or tourist tree, Burseraceae; tropical America, photographed in Costa Rica.

Buxus sempervirens, common boxwood, Buxaceae; Europe, photographed in the Dublin Botanical Garden, Ireland.

Calocedrus decurrens, incense cedar, Cupressaceae; western North America, photographed in the Forest Trial Garden, Grafrath, Germany.

Calocedrus decurrens, incense cedar, Cupressaceae; western North America, photographed in the vicinity of Bienne, Switzerland.

Carica papaya, papaya, Caricaceae; tropical America, photographed in the Shandrani Hotel Park, Mauritius.

Carpinus betulus, European hornbeam, Betulaceae; Europe, photographed in the vicinity of Bienne, Switzerland.

Carpinus betulus, European hornbeam, Betulaceae; Europe, photographed in the Munich Botanical Garden, Germany.

Carya illinoinensis, pecan, Juglandaceae; southeastern North America, photographed in the Padua Botanical Garden, Italy.

Carya laciniosa, shellbark hickory, Juglandaceae; eastern North America, photographed in
the Munich Botanical Garden, Germany.

Carya ovata, shagbark hickory, Juglandaceae;
eastern North America, photographed in the
Forest Trial Garden, Grafrath, Germany.

Carya tomentosa, mockernut hickory, Juglandaceae; eastern North America, photographed in
the Royal Botanic Gardens, Kew, England.

Castanea sativa, sweet chestnut, Fagaceae;
western Eurasia, photographed in the Royal
Botanic Gardens, Kew, England.

Casuarina equisetifolia, Australian pine, Casuarinaceae; coastal eastern Australia, photographed on the Canary Islands, Spain.

Casuarina equisetifolia, Australian pine, Casuarinaceae; coastal eastern Australia, photographed in the Shandrani Hotel Park, Mauritius.

Casuarina torulosa, rose she-oak, Casuarinaceae; eastern Australia, photographed in the University of California, Berkeley, Botanical Garden.

Catalpa bignonioides, southern catalpa, Bignoniaceae; southeastern North America, photographed in the Royal Botanic Gardens, Kew, England.

Catalpa speciosa, northern catalpa, Bignoniaceae; eastern North America, photographed in
the Geneva Botanical Garden, Switzerland.

Catalpa speciosa, northern catalpa, Bignoniaceae; eastern North America, photographed in
the Geneva Botanical Garden, Switzerland.

Cedrus deodara, deodar cedar, Pinaceae; Himalaya, photographed in northern Italy.

Cedrus libani subsp. *atlantica,* Atlas cedar,
Pinaceae; northwestern Africa, photographed
on the Canary Islands, Spain.

Cedrus libani subsp. *brevifolia,* Cyprus cedar, Pinaceae; eastern Mediterranean region, photographed in the vicinity of Neuchâtel, Switzerland.

Cedrus libani subsp. *brevifolia,* Cyprus cedar, Pinaceae; eastern Mediterranean region, photographed in the Arboretum des Barres, Nogent-sur-Vernisson, France.

Cedrus libani subsp. *libani,* cedar of Lebanon, Pinaceae; eastern Mediterranean region, photographed in the St. Gall Botanical Garden, Switzerland.

Cedrus libani subsp. *libani,* cedar of Lebanon, Pinaceae; eastern Mediterranean region, photographed in the vicinity of Orléans, France.

Celtis australis, European nettle tree, Celtidaceae; southern Europe, photographed in the vicinity of Bienne, Switzerland.

Celtis caucasica, Caucasian nettle tree, Celtidaceae; southwestern Asia, photographed in the Royal Botanic Gardens, Kew, England.

Celtis jessoensis, Japanese nettle tree, Celtidaceae; eastern Asia, photographed in the Arboretum des Barres, Nogent-sur-Vernisson, France.

Celtis occidentalis, hackberry, Celtidaceae; eastern North America, photographed in the Padua Botanical Garden, Italy.

Cercidiphyllum japonicum, katsura tree, Cercidiphyllaceae; eastern Asia, photographed in the Bern Botanical Garden, Switzerland.

Cercidiphyllum japonicum var. *magnificum,* big-leaf katsura tree, Cercidiphyllaceae; eastern Asia, photographed on Mainau Island, Lake Constance, Germany.

Cercis racemosa, pale Chinese redbud, Leguminosae; eastern Asia, photographed in the Hillier Arboretum, England.

Cercis siliquastrum, Judas tree, Leguminosae; southern Europe, photographed in northern Italy.

Chamaecyparis lawsoniana, Port Orford cedar, Cupressaceae; western North America, photographed in a national forest in Oregon.

Chamaecyparis lawsoniana, Port Orford cedar, Cupressaceae; western North America, photographed in the Forest Trial Garden, Grafrath, Germany.

Chamaecyparis lawsoniana, Port Orford cedar, Cupressaceae; western North America, photographed on Mainau Island, Lake Constance, Germany.

Chamaecyparis pisifera, sawara cypress, Cupressaceae; eastern Asia, photographed in the Padua Botanical Garden, Italy.

Chamaerops humilis, European fan palm, Palmae; western Mediterranean region, photographed in northern Italy.

Chorisia speciosa, silk floss tree, Malvaceae; eastern South
America, photographed in Wisley Garden, England.

Chorisia speciosa, silk floss tree, Malvaceae; eastern South America, photographed in the Orotava Acclimatization Garden, Tenerife, Spain.

Cinnamomum camphora, camphor tree, Lauraceae; southeastern Asia, photographed in the Thuret Garden, Cap d'Antibes, France.

Citrus aurantium, sour orange, Rutaceae; eastern Asia, photographed in Cap Ferrat on the Côte d'Azur, France.

Clerodendrum trichotomum, chance tree, Verbenaceae; eastern Asia, photographed in the Padua Botanical Garden, Italy.

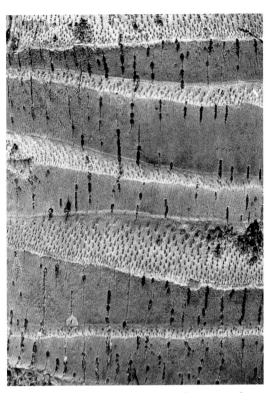

Cocos nucifera, coconut palm, Palmae; south-western Pacific, photographed in Costa Rica.

Cocos nucifera, coconut palm, Palmae; south-western Pacific, photographed in the Shandrani Hotel Park, Mauritius.

Cornus alba 'Sibirica', Siberian red osier, Cornaceae; northern Eurasia, photographed in the vicinity of Bienne, Switzerland.

Cornus macrophylla, big-leaf dogwood, Cornaceae; eastern Asia, photographed in the Dublin Botanical Garden, Ireland.

Cornus mas, cornelian cherry, Cornaceae; Europe, photographed in a park in Geneva, Switzerland.

Corylus colurna, Turkish hazel, Betulaceae; southwestern Asia,
photographed on Mainau Island, Lake Constance, Germany.

Corylus colurna, Turkish hazel, Betulaceae; southwestern Asia, photographed on Mainau Island, Lake Constance, Germany.

Cotinus coggygria 'Purpureus', European smoke tree, Anacardiaceae; southern Eurasia, photographed in the Arboretum des Barres, Nogent-sur-Vernisson, France.

Cotinus obovatus, American smoke tree, Anacardiaceae; southeastern North America, photographed in the Royal Botanic Gardens, Kew, England.

Crataegus 'Blue Hawthorn', Rosaceae; eastern North America, photographed in the Agricultural Experiment Station, Aurora, Washington.

Crataegus caesa, Michigan hawthorn, Rosaceae; northeastern North America, photographed in the Royal Botanic Gardens, Kew, England.

Crataegus pinnatifida, Chinese hawthorn, Rosaceae; eastern Asia, photographed in the Van Dusen Botanical Garden, Vancouver, Canada.

Crataegus tanacetifolia, Asian hawthorn, Rosaceae; eastern Asia, photographed at Malahide Castle, Ireland.

Cryptocarya rubra, Chilean laurel, Lauraceae; southern South America, photographed in the Strybing Arboretum, San Francisco, California.

Cryptomeria japonica, sugi, Cupressaceae; eastern Asia, photographed in the Villa Pallavicino Park, Stresa, Italy.

Cryptomeria japonica, sugi, Cupressaceae; eastern Asia, photographed in the Villa Pallavicino Park, Stresa, Italy.

Cryptomeria japonica, sugi, Cupressaceae; eastern Asia, photographed in the Villa Pallavicino Park, Stresa, Italy.

Cunninghamia lanceolata, China fir, Cupressaceae; eastern Asia, photographed in the Arboretum des Barres, Nogent-sur-Vernisson, France.

Cunninghamia lanceolata, China fir, Cupressaceae; eastern Asia, photographed in the Washington Park Arboretum, Seattle, Washington.

109

Cupressus arizonica, Arizona cypress, Cupressaceae; southwestern North America, photographed at Powerscourt, Ireland.

Cupressus arizonica 'Pyramidalis', upright Arizona cypress, Cupressaceae; southwestern North America, photographed in northern Italy.

Cupressus arizonica var. *glabra,* smooth Arizona cypress, Cupressaceae; southwestern North America, photographed in the Tropical Botanical Garden, Lisbon, Portugal.

Cupressus guadalupensis, Guadalupe cypress, Cupressaceae; northwestern Mexico, photographed in the Thuret Garden, Cap d'Antibes, France.

Cupressus lusitanica, cedar of Goa, Cupressaceae; Central America, photographed in the Thuret Garden, Cap d'Antibes, France.

Cupressus macrocarpa, Monterey cypress, Cupressaceae; coastal
California, photographed in the Strybing Arboretum, San Francisco.

Cupressus macrocarpa, Monterey cypress, Cupressaceae; coastal California, photographed by Monterey Bay.

Cupressus macrocarpa, Monterey cypress, Cupressaceae; coastal California, photographed by Monterey Bay.

Cupressus nootkatensis 'Pendula', weeping Alaska yellow cedar, Cupressaceae; northwestern North America, photographed in the Dublin Botanical Garden, Ireland.

Cupressus sempervirens, Mediterranean cypress, Cupressaceae; Mediterranean region, photographed in the Jardin des Plantes, Montpellier, France.

Cupressus sempervirens, Mediterranean cypress, Cupressaceae; Mediterranean region, photographed in the Jardin des Plantes, Montpellier, France.

Cupressus torulosa, Himalayan cypress, Cupressaceae; Himalaya, photographed in the Padua Botanical Garden, Italy.

Cyathea australis, Australian rough tree fern, Cyatheaceae; eastern Australia, photographed in the Royal Botanic Gardens, Kew, England.

Dacrydium cupressinum, rimu, New Zealand red pine, Podocarpaceae; New Zealand, photographed in the Strybing Arboretum, San Francisco, California.

Davidia involucrata, dove tree, Cornaceae; eastern Asia, photographed on Isola Madre, Lake Maggiore, Italy.

Davidia involucrata 'Vilmoriniana', dove tree, Cornaceae; eastern Asia, photographed in the Vallon d'Aubonne Arboretum, Vaud, Switzerland.

Diospyros kaki, Japanese persimmon, Ebenaceae; eastern Asia, photographed in the Padua Botanical Garden, Italy.

Diospyros kaki 'Mazelii', Japanese persimmon, Ebenaceae; eastern Asia, photographed in the Padua Botanical Garden, Italy.

Diospyros lotus, date plum, Ebenaceae; eastern Asia, photographed in the Royal Botanic Gardens, Kew, England.

Diospyros virginiana, common persimmon, Ebenaceae; eastern North America, photographed in the Royal Botanic Gardens, Kew, England.

Dipelta floribunda, dipelta, Caprifoliaceae; eastern Asia, photographed in the Neuchâtel Botanical Garden, Switzerland.

Dracaena draco, dragon tree, Agavaceae; Canary Islands, photographed in the Munich Botanical Garden, Germany.

Ehretia dicksonii, large-leaf heliotrope tree, Boraginaceae; eastern
Asia, photographed in the Royal Botanic Gardens, Kew, England.

Ehretia dicksonii, large-leaf heliotrope tree, Boraginaceae; eastern Asia, photographed in the Royal Botanic Gardens, Kew, England.

Elaeagnus angustifolia, Russian olive, Elaeagnaceae; western Asia, photographed in the Neuchâtel Botanical Garden, Switzerland.

Erica arborea, tree heath, Ericaceae; Mediterranean region, photographed on the Canary Islands, Spain.

Erythrina carnea, fleshy coral tree, Leguminosae; South America, photographed in the Orotava Acclimatization Garden, Tenerife, Spain.

Erythrina abyssinica, red-hot-poker tree, Leguminosae; tropical Africa,
photographed in the Kirstenbosch National Botanical Garden, South Africa.

Erythrina corallodendron, coral tree, Leguminosae; West Indies, photographed in the Orotava Acclimatization Garden, Tenerife, Spain.

Erythrina corallodendron, coral tree, Leguminosae; West Indies, photographed in the Orotava Acclimatization Garden, Tenerife, Spain.

Erythrina velutina, velvet coral tree, Leguminosae; northern South America, photographed in the Orotava Acclimatization Garden, Tenerife, Spain.

Eucalyptus blakelyi, Blakely's red gum, Myrtaceae; southeastern Australia, photographed in the University of California, Berkeley, Botanical Garden.

Eucalyptus caesia, gungurru, Myrtaceae; western Australia, photographed in the University of California, Santa Cruz, Arboretum.

Eucalyptus camaldulensis, river red gum, Myrtaceae; Australia, photographed in the Thuret Garden, Cap d'Antibes, France.

Eucalyptus cephalocarpa, mealy stringybark, Myrtaceae; southeastern Australia, photographed in the Esterel Arboretum, Côte d'Azur, France.

Eucalyptus coccifera, Tasmanian snow gum, Myrtaceae; Tasmania, photographed in Mount Usher Gardens, Ireland.

Eucalyptus dalrympleana, mountain gum, Myrtaceae; southeastern Australia, photographed in the Royal Botanic Gardens, Kew, England.

Eucalyptus deglupta, Mindanao gum, Myrtaceae; East Indies, photographed in the Durban Botanical Garden, South Africa.

Eucalyptus deglupta, Mindanao gum, Myrtaceae; East Indies, photographed in the Durban Botanical Garden, South Africa.

Eucalyptus delegatensis, woolly butt, Myrtaceae; southeastern Australia, photographed in Mount Usher Gardens, Ireland.

Eucalyptus ficifolia, red-flowering gum, Myrtaceae; western Australia, photographed in the Strybing Arboretum, San Francisco, California.

Eucalyptus glaucescens, Tingaringy gum, Myrtaceae; southeastern Australia, photographed in the Royal Botanic Gardens, Kew, England.

Eucalyptus globulus, blue gum, Myrtaceae; southeastern Australia, photographed in the Hanbury Garden, La Mortola, Italy.

Eucalyptus grandis, rose gum, Myrtaceae; eastern Australia, photographed in the Transvaal, South Africa.

Eucalyptus gunnii, cider gum, Myrtaceae; Tasmania, photographed at Dunloe Castle Hotel Garden, Ireland.

Eucalyptus haematoxylon, mountain marri, Myrtaceae; southwestern Australia, photographed in the University of California, Santa Cruz, Arboretum.

Eucalyptus laeliae, powder-bark wandoo, Myrtaceae; southwestern Australia, photographed in the University of California, Santa Cruz, Arboretum.

Eucalyptus maculata, spotted gum, Myrtaceae; eastern Australia, photographed in the Thuret Garden, Cap d'Antibes, France.

Eucalyptus microcorys, Australian tallow wood, Myrtaceae; eastern Australia, photographed in the Hanbury Garden, La Mortola, Italy.

Eucalyptus parvifolia, small-leaved gum, Myrtaceae; southeastern Australia, photographed at Fota House, Ireland.

Eucalyptus pauciflora, white sallee, Myrtaceae; southeastern Australia, photographed on the Côte d'Azur, France.

Eucalyptus pauciflora, white sallee, Myrtaceae; southeastern Australia, photographed in Wisley Garden, England.

Eucalyptus pauciflora subsp. *niphophila,* snow gum, Myrtaceae; southeastern Australia, photographed in the Agricultural Experiment Station, Aurora, Washington.

Eucalyptus pauciflora subsp. *niphophila,* snow gum, Myrtaceae; southeastern Australia, photographed at Dunloe Castle Hotel Garden, Ireland.

Eucalyptus regnans, Australian mountain ash, Myrtaceae; southeastern Australia, photographed in Mount Usher Gardens, Ireland.

Eucalyptus urnigera, urn gum, Myrtaceae; Tasmania, photographed in Wisley Garden, England.

Eucalyptus urnigera, urn gum, Myrtaceae; Tasmania, photographed in Mount Usher Gardens, Ireland.

Eucalyptus viminalis, manna gum, Myrtaceae; southeastern Australia, photographed in the Thuret Garden, Cap d'Antibes, France.

Fagus orientalis, Caucasian beech, Fagaceae; southwestern Asia, photographed in the Van Dusen Botanical Garden, Vancouver, Canada.

Fagus sylvatica, European beech, Fagaceae; Europe, photographed in the Swiss Jura.

Fagus sylvatica, European beech, Fagaceae; Europe, photographed at Mount Congreve, Ireland.

Fagus sylvatica, European beech, Fagaceae; Europe, photographed at Hof ter Saksen, Belgium.

Ficus benjamina, weeping fig, Moraceae; southeastern Asia, photographed on the Canary Islands, Spain.

Ficus carica, common fig, Moraceae; southwestern Asia, photographed on the Canary Islands, Spain.

Ficus microcarpa, Indian laurel, Moraceae; southeastern Asia, photographed on the Canary Islands, Spain.

Firmiana simplex, Chinese parasol tree, Malvaceae; eastern Asia, photographed in the Padua Botanical Garden, Italy.

Fraxinus americana, white ash, Oleaceae; eastern North America, photographed in the Padua Botanical Garden, Italy.

Fraxinus angustifolia, narrow-leaved ash, Oleaceae; southern Europe, photographed in the Royal Botanic Gardens, Kew, England.

Fraxinus excelsior, common European ash, Oleaceae; Europe, photographed in the Swiss Alps.

Fraxinus excelsior, common European ash, Oleaceae; Europe, photographed in the Swiss Jura.

Fraxinus latifolia, Oregon ash, Oleaceae; western North America, photographed in the Royal Botanic Gardens, Kew, England.

Fraxinus mandshurica, Manchurian ash, Oleaceae; eastern Asia, photographed in the Vallon d'Aubonne Arboretum, Vaud, Switzerland.

Fraxinus pennsylvanica, green ash, Oleaceae; eastern North America, photographed in the Royal Botanic Gardens, Kew, England.

Ginkgo biloba, ginkgo or maidenhair tree, Ginkgoaceae; eastern Asia, photographed in the Padua Botanical Garden, Italy.

Ginkgo biloba, ginkgo or maidenhair tree, Ginkgoaceae; eastern Asia, photographed on Isola Madre, Lake Maggiore, Italy.

Gleditsia aquatica, water locust, Leguminosae; southeastern North America, photographed in the Geneva Botanical Garden, Switzerland.

Gleditsia japonica, Japanese honey locust, Leguminosae; eastern Asia, photographed in the Padua Botanical Garden, Italy.

Gleditsia triacanthos, honey locust, Leguminosae; eastern North America, photographed in the Forest Trial Garden, Grafrath, Germany.

Grevillea robusta, silky oak, Proteaceae; eastern Australia, photographed in the Thuret Garden, Cap d'Antibes, France.

Gymnocladus dioicus, Kentucky coffee tree, Leguminosae; eastern North America, photographed in the Padua Botanical Garden, Italy.

Gymnocladus dioicus, Kentucky coffee tree, Leguminosae; eastern North America, photographed in the Padua Botanical Garden, Italy.

Halesia carolina, Carolina silverbell, Styracaceae; southeastern North America, photographed in the Washington Park Arboretum, Seattle, Washington.

Hovenia dulcis, Japanese raisin tree, Rhamnaceae; eastern Asia, photographed in the Geneva Botanical Garden, Switzerland.

Idesia polycarpa, iigiri tree, Flacourtiaceae; eastern Asia, photographed in the University of British Columbia Botanical Garden, Vancouver, Canada.

Ilex aquifolium, English holly, Aquifoliaceae; Europe, photographed in the Royal Botanic Gardens, Kew, England.

Ilex chinensis, Chinese holly, Aquifoliaceae; eastern Asia, photographed in the Washington Park Arboretum, Seattle, Washington.

Ilex ciliospinosa, minispined holly, Aquifoliaceae; eastern Asia, photographed in the Washington Park Arboretum, Seattle, Washington.

Ilex integra, mochi holly, Aquifoliaceae; eastern Asia, photographed in the Washington Park Arboretum, Seattle, Washington.

Jacaranda mimosifolia, common jacaranda, Bignoniaceae; central South America, photographed on the Canary Islands, Spain.

Jubaea chilensis, Chilean wine palm, Palmae; southern South America, photographed in the Thuret Garden, Cap d'Antibes, France.

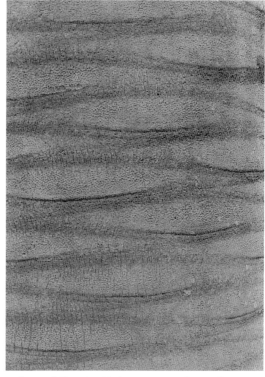

Jubaea chilensis, Chilean wine palm, Palmae; southern South America, photographed in the Thuret Garden, Cap d'Antibes, France.

Jubaea chilensis, Chilean wine palm, Palmae; southern South America, photographed in the Thuret Garden, Cap d'Antibes, France.

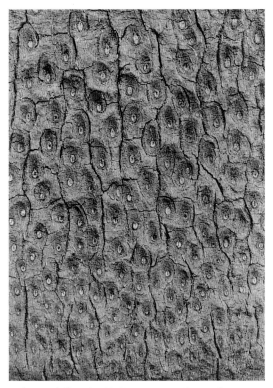

Jubaea chilensis, Chilean wine palm, Palmae; southern South America, photographed in the Thuret Garden, Cap d'Antibes, France.

Juglans ailantifolia, heart nut, Juglandaceae; eastern Asia, photographed in the Forest Trial Garden, Grafrath, Germany.

Juglans ×intermedia, hybrid walnut, Juglandaceae; originated in cultivation, photographed in the Padua Botanical Garden, Italy.

Juglans nigra, black walnut, Juglandaceae; eastern North America, photographed on Mainau Island, Lake Constance, Germany.

Juglans regia, Persian walnut, Juglandaceae; southern central Eurasia, photographed in Hemelrijk, Belgium.

Juniperus cedrus, Canary Island juniper, Cupressaceae; Canary Islands, photographed on the Canary Islands, Spain.

Juniperus chinensis, Chinese juniper, Cupressaceae; eastern Asia, photographed in the Royal Botanic Gardens, Kew, England.

Juniperus deppeana, alligator juniper, Cupressaceae; southwestern North America, photographed in the Geneva Botanical Garden, Switzerland.

Juniperus oxycedrus, prickly juniper, Cupressaceae; Mediterranean region, photographed in the Geneva Botanical Garden, Switzerland.

Juniperus recurva, Himalayan weeping juniper, Cupressaceae; Himalaya, photographed at Birr Castle, Ireland.

Juniperus virginiana, eastern red cedar, Cupressaceae; eastern North America, photographed in the Royal Botanic Gardens, Kew, England.

Kalopanax septemlobus, tree aralia, Araliaceae; eastern Asia, photographed in the St. Gall Botanical Garden, Switzerland.

Koelreuteria bipinnata, Chinese lantern tree, Sapindaceae; eastern Asia, photographed in the Hanbury Garden, La Mortola, Italy.

Koelreuteria paniculata, golden rain tree, Sapindaceae; eastern Asia, photographed in the Royal Botanic Gardens, Kew, England.

Laburnum anagyroides 'Damazia', golden chain tree, Leguminosae; Europe, photographed in the Padua Botanical Garden, Italy.

Laburnum ×watereri 'Vossii', hybrid golden chain tree, Leguminosae; originated in cultivation, photographed in the Van Dusen Botanical Garden, Vancouver, Canada.

Laburnum sp., laburnum, Leguminosae; Europe,
photographed at Birr Castle, Ireland.

146

Lagerstroemia indica, crape myrtle, Lythraceae; southeastern Asia, photographed in the Shandrani Hotel Park, Mauritius.

Larix decidua, European larch, Pinaceae; Europe, photographed in the Swiss Alps.

Larix decidua, European larch, Pinaceae; Europe, photographed in the Swiss Alps.

Larix decidua, European larch, Pinaceae; Europe, photographed in the Swiss Alps.

Larix ×eurokurilensis, larch, Pinaceae; originated in cultivation, photographed in the Forest Trial Garden, Grafrath, Germany.

Larix gmelinii, Dahurian larch, Pinaceae; northeastern Asia, photographed in the Hoyt Arboretum, Portland, Oregon.

Larix gmelinii, Dahurian larch, Pinaceae; northeastern Asia, photographed in the Geneva Botanical Garden, Switzerland.

Larix kaempferi, Japanese larch, Pinaceae; Japan, photographed on Mainau Island, Lake Constance, Germany.

Larix occidentalis, western larch, Pinaceae; western North America, photographed in the Arboretum des Barres, Nogent-sur-Vernisson, France.

Laurus azorica, Canary laurel, Lauraceae; Macaronesia, photographed on the Canary Islands, Spain.

Leucadendron argenteum, silver tree, Proteaceae; South Africa, photographed in the Strybing Arboretum, San Francisco, California.

Leucadendron argenteum, silver tree, Proteaceae; South Africa, photographed in the Kirstenbosch National Botanical Garden, South Africa.

Liquidambar styraciflua, sweet gum, Hamamel-idaceae; southeastern North America, photographed in northern Italy.

Liriodendron chinense, Chinese tulip tree, Magnoliaceae; eastern Asia, photographed in the Royal Botanic Gardens, Kew, England.

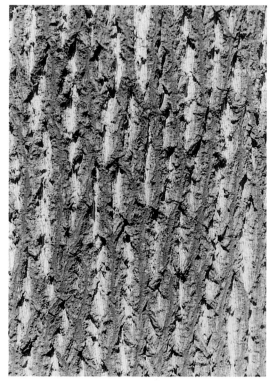

Liriodendron tulipifera, tulip tree, Magnolia-ceae; eastern North America, photographed in the Padua Botanical Garden, Italy.

Liriodendron tulipifera, tulip tree, Magnoliaceae; eastern North America, photographed in the Strybing Arboretum, San Francisco, California.

Lithocarpus densiflorus, tanoak, Fagaceae; western North America, photographed in Redwood National Park, California.

Luma apiculata, arrayán myrtle, Myrtaceae; southern South America, photographed at Dunloe Castle Hotel Garden, Ireland.

Maclura pomifera, Osage orange, Moraceae; southeastern North America, photographed in the Orotava Acclimatization Garden, Tenerife, Spain.

Magnolia acuminata, cucumber tree, Magnoliaceae; eastern North America, photographed in the Royal Botanic Gardens, Kew, England.

Magnolia campbellii, Himalayan magnolia, Magnoliaceae; Himalaya, photographed in the Strybing Arboretum, San Francisco, California.

Magnolia grandiflora, southern magnolia or bull bay, Magnoliaceae; southeastern North America, photographed in the Padua Botanical Garden, Italy.

Magnolia hypoleuca, Japanese silverleaf magnolia, Magnoliaceae; eastern Asia, photographed in the Padua Botanical Garden, Italy.

Magnolia nitida, Tibetan glossy magnolia, Magnoliaceae, Himalaya, photographed at Malahide Castle, Ireland.

Magnolia ×veitchii, Veitch magnolia, Magnoliaceae; originated in cultivation, photographed in the Strybing Arboretum, San Francisco, California. Holes drilled by sapsuckers.

Malus ×domestica, orchard apple, Rosaceae; Europe, photographed in the vicinity of Bienne, Switzerland.

Malus ×domestica, orchard apple, Rosaceae; Europe, photographed in the vicinity of Bienne, Switzerland.

Melaleuca styphelioides, heath-leaf paperbark, Myrtaceae; eastern Australia, photographed in the Thuret Garden, Cap d'Antibes, France.

Melaleuca styphelioides, heath-leaf paperbark, Myrtaceae; eastern Australia, photographed in the Thuret Garden, Cap d'Antibes, France.

Melia azederach, China berry, Meliaceae; Himalaya, photographed in the Geneva Botanical Garden, Switzerland.

Melia azederach 'Floribunda', China berry, Meliaceae; Himalaya, photographed in the Menton Botanical Garden, France.

Mespilus germanica, medlar, Rosaceae; Europe, photographed in the Zürich Botanical Garden, Switzerland.

Metasequoia glyptostroboides, dawn redwood, Cupressaceae; eastern Asia, photographed in the Bern Botanical Garden, Switzerland.

Metasequoia glyptostroboides, dawn redwood, Cupressaceae; eastern Asia, photographed on Mainau Island, Lake Constance, Germany.

Morus alba, white mulberry, Moraceae; eastern Asia, photographed in the Padua Botanical Garden, Italy.

Morus alba, white mulberry, Moraceae; eastern Asia, photographed in the Bern Botanical Garden, Switzerland.

Morus bombycis, sycamore mulberry, Moraceae; eastern Asia,
photographed in the Dublin Botanical Garden, Ireland.

Morus cathayana, Chinese black mulberry, Moraceae; eastern
Asia, photographed in the Royal Botanic Gardens, Kew, England.

Morus nigra, black mulberry, Moraceae; southwestern Asia, photographed in the Royal Botanic Gardens, Kew, England.

Myrica faya, Canary Island bayberry, Myricaceae; Mascarene Islands, photographed on the Canary Islands, Spain.

Nothofagus antarctica, nire beech, Nothofagaceae; southern South America, photographed in the Geneva Botanical Garden, Switzerland.

Nothofagus obliqua, roble beech, Nothofagaceae; southern South America, photographed in the Royal Botanic Gardens, Kew, England.

Nothofagus menziesii, silver beech, Nothofagaceae; New
Zealand, photographed at Mount Usher Gardens, Ireland.

Nothofagus solandri var. *cliffortioides*, mountain beech, Nothofagaceae; New Zealand, photographed in the Hillier Arboretum, England.

Olea europea, common olive, Oleaceae; Mediterranean region, photographed in the Padua Botanical Garden, Italy.

Olea europea, common olive, Oleaceae; Mediterranean region, photographed in the Hanbury Garden, La Mortola, Italy.

Ostrya carpinifolia, hop hornbeam, Betulaceae; southwestern Eurasia, photographed in northern Italy.

Ostrya japonica, Japanese hop hornbeam, Betulaceae; eastern Asia, photographed in the Royal Botanic Gardens, Kew, England.

Ostrya virginiana, eastern ironwood or eastern hop hornbeam, Betulaceae; eastern North America, photographed in the Royal Botanic Gardens, Kew, England.

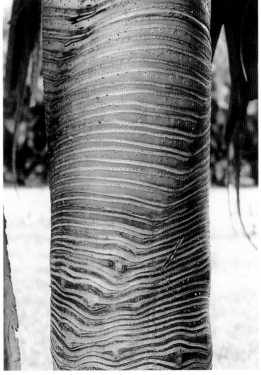

Pachypodium geayi, Apocynaceae; Madagascar, photographed in the Bonn Botanical Garden, Germany.

Pandanus utilis, screw pine, Pandanaceae; Madagascar, photographed in the Pamplemousses Botanical Garden, Mauritius.

161

Parrotia persica, Persian ironwood, Hamamelidaceae; southwest-ern Asia, photographed in the vicinity of Bienne, Switzerland.

Parrotia persica, Persian ironwood, Hamamelidaceae; southwestern Asia, photographed in the Royal Botanic Gardens, Kew, England.

Paulownia tomentosa, princess tree, Scrophulariaceae; eastern Asia, photographed in the Padua Botanical Garden, Italy.

Paxistima myrtifolia, Oregon boxwood, Celastraceae; western North America, photographed in the University of California, Berkeley, Botanical Garden.

Pereskia grandifolia, rose cactus, Cactaceae; eastern South America, photographed in the Royal Botanic Gardens, Kew, England.

163

Phellodendron amurense, Amur cork tree, Rutaceae; eastern Asia, photographed on Mainau Island, Lake Constance, Germany.

Phillyrea latifolia, mock privet, Oleaceae; Mediterranean region, photographed in the Jardin des Plantes, Montpellier, France.

Phoenix dactylifera, date palm, Palmae; Mediterranean region, photographed in Cannes, France.

Phoenix dactylifera, date palm, Palmae; Mediterranean region, photographed in the Orotava Acclimatization Garden, Tenerife, Spain.

Picea abies, Norway spruce, Pinaceae; Europe, photographed in the Swiss Jura.

Picea asperata, dragon spruce, Pinaceae; eastern Asia, photographed in the Royal Botanic Gardens, Kew, England.

166

Picea engelmannii, Engelmann spruce, Pinaceae; western North America, photographed in the Rocky Mountains, British Columbia, Canada.

Picea glauca, white spruce, Pinaceae; northern North America, photographed in the Rocky Mountains, British Columbia, Canada.

Picea likiangensis, Lijiang spruce, Pinaceae; eastern Asia, photographed in the Royal Botanic Gardens, Kew, England.

Picea omorika, Serbian spruce, Pinaceae; southeastern Europe, photographed in the Royal Botanic Gardens, Kew, England.

Picea orientalis, Caucasian spruce, Pinaceae; southwestern Asia, photographed in the Royal Botanic Gardens, Kew, England.

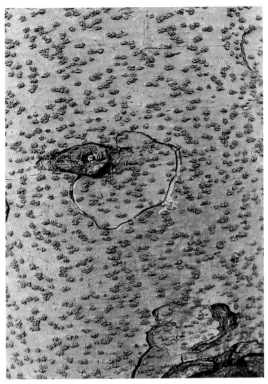

Picea orientalis, Caucasian spruce, Pinaceae; southwestern Asia, photographed in the Royal Botanic Gardens, Kew, England.

Picea polita, tigertail spruce, Pinaceae; eastern Asia, photographed in the Hoyt Arboretum, Portland, Oregon.

Picea pungens 'Glauca', Colorado blue spruce, Pinaceae; western North America, photographed in the Arboretum des Barres, Nogent-sur-Vernisson, France.

Picea sitchensis, Sitka spruce, Pinaceae; western North America, photographed on the Olympic Peninsula, Washington.

Pinus armandii, Chinese white pine, Pinaceae; eastern Asia, photographed in the Arboretum des Barres, Nogent-sur-Vernisson, France.

Pinus armandii, Chinese white pine, Pinaceae; eastern Asia, photographed in the Royal Botanic Gardens, Kew, England.

Pinus banksiana, jack pine, Pinaceae; northern North America, photographed in the Geneva Botanical Garden, Switzerland.

Pinus bungeana, lacebark pine, Pinaceae; eastern Asia, photographed in the Thuret Garden, Cap d'Antibes, France.

Pinus bungeana, lacebark pine, Pinaceae; eastern Asia,
photographed in the Royal Botanic Gardens, Kew, England.

Pinus bungeana, lacebark pine, Pinaceae; eastern Asia, photographed in the Royal Botanic Gardens, Kew, England.

Pinus canariensis, Canary Island pine, Pinaceae; Canary Islands, photographed in the Thuret Garden, Cap d'Antibes, France.

Pinus cembra, arolla pine, Pinaceae; southern Europe, photographed in the Swiss Alps.

Pinus cembra, arolla pine, Pinaceae; southern Europe, photographed in the Engadine, Switzerland. See also p. 174.

172

Pinus canariensis, Canary Island pine, Pinaceae; Canary
Islands, photographed on the Canary Islands, Spain.

Pinus cembra, arolla pine, Pinaceae; southern
Europe, photographed at St. Moritz, Switzerland.

Pinus contorta, lodgepole pine, Pinaceae; western North America, photographed in the Rocky Mountains, British Columbia, Canada.

Pinus contorta var. *bolanderi,* Pygmy Forest pine, Pinaceae; western North America, photographed in Van Damme (Pygmy Forest) State Park, California.

Pinus coulteri, Coulter pine, Pinaceae; western North America, photographed in the Thuret Garden, Cap d'Antibes, France.

Pinus densiflora, Japanese red pine, Pinaceae; eastern Asia, photographed in the English Gardens, Seattle, Washington.

Pinus flexilis, limber pine, Pinaceae; western North America, photographed in the Forest Trial Garden, Grafrath, Germany.

Pinus halepensis, Aleppo pine, Pinaceae; Mediterranean region, photographed on the Côte d'Azur, France.

Pinus halepensis, Aleppo pine, Pinaceae; Mediterranean region, photographed on the Côte d'Azur, France.

Pinus halepensis subsp. *brutia*, Calabrian pine, Pinaceae; Mediterranean region, photographed in the Orotava Acclimatization Garden, Tenerife, Spain.

Pinus jeffreyi, Jeffrey pine, Pinaceae; western North
America, photographed in a national forest in Oregon.

Pinus jeffreyi, Jeffrey pine, Pinaceae; western North America, photographed on Mainau Island, Lake Constance, Germany.

Pinus koraiensis, Korean white pine, Pinaceae; eastern Asia, photographed at Fota House, Ireland.

Pinus montezumae, Montezuma's pine, Pinaceae; Mexico, photographed at Fota House, Ireland.

Pinus monticola, western white pine, Pinaceae; western North America, photographed in Mount Rainier National Park, Washington.

Pinus monticola, western white pine, Pinaceae; western North America, photographed in Mount Rainier National Park, Washington.

Pinus mugo, mugo pine, Pinaceae; southern Europe, photographed in the Swiss Alps.

Pinus nigra, Austrian black pine, Pinaceae; southwestern Eurasia, photographed in the Royal Botanic Gardens, Kew, England.

Pinus nigra, Austrian black pine, Pinaceae; southwestern Eurasia, photographed in the Royal Botanic Gardens, Kew, England.

Pinus nigra, Austrian black pine, Pinaceae; southwestern Eurasia, photographed in the Padua Botanical Garden, Italy.

Pinus parviflora, Japanese white pine, Pinaceae; eastern Asia, photographed in the Royal Botanic Gardens, Kew, England.

Pinus parviflora, Japanese white pine, Pinaceae; eastern Asia, photographed in the Royal Botanic Gardens, Kew, England.

Pinus patula, eastern Mexican weeping pine, Pinaceae; Mexico, photographed in the University of California, Berkeley, Botanical Garden.

Pinus pinaster subsp. *atlantica,* maritime pine, Pinaceae; western Mediterranean region, photographed near Capbreton, Aquitaine, France.

Pinus pinaster, maritime pine, Pinaceae; western Mediterranean region, photographed in the Royal Botanic Gardens, Kew, England.

Pinus pinea, Mediterranean stone pine, Pinaceae; Mediterranean region, photographed in northern Italy.

Pinus pinea, Mediterranean stone pine, Pinaceae; Mediterranean region, photographed in the Royal Botanic Gardens, Kew, England.

Pinus ponderosa, ponderosa pine, western yellow pine, Pinaceae; western North America, photographed in the Rocky Mountains, British Columbia, Canada.

Pinus radiata, Monterey pine, Pinaceae; south-western North America, photographed on the Canary Islands, Spain.

Pinus radiata, Monterey pine, Pinaceae; south-western North America, photographed in Muck-ross Gardens, Ireland.

Pinus radiata, Monterey pine, Pinaceae; south-western North America, photographed by Mon-terey Bay, California.

Pinus resinosa, eastern red pine, Pinaceae; northeastern North America, photographed in the Royal Botanic Gardens, Kew, England.

Pinus resinosa, eastern red pine, Pinaceae; northeastern North America, photographed in the Royal Botanic Gardens, Kew, England.

Pinus rigida, pitch pine, Pinaceae; eastern North America, photographed in Wakehurst Place Garden, England.

Pinus roxburghii, chir pine, Pinaceae; Himalaya, photographed in the Thuret Garden, Cap d'Antibes, France.

Pinus strobus, eastern white pine, Pinaceae; eastern North America, photographed in the Washington Park Arboretum, Seattle, Washington.

184

Pinus sabiniana, gray pine, Pinaceae; southwestern North America, photographed in Montriant Park, Geneva, Switzerland.

Pinus sylvestris, Scots pine, Pinaceae; Eurasia, photographed in the vicinity of Bienne, Switzerland.

Pinus sylvestris, Scots pine, Pinaceae; Eurasia, photographed in Muckross Gardens, Ireland.

Pinus sylvestris var. *engadinensis*, Scots pine, Pinaceae; Eurasia, photographed in the Swiss Alps.

Pinus torreyana, Torrey pine, Pinaceae; southwestern North America, photographed in the Strybing Arboretum, San Francisco, California.

Pinus wallichiana, Himalayan white pine, Pinaceae; Himalaya, photographed in the vicinity of Tessin, Switzerland.

Pistacia terebinthus, Cyprus turpentine shrub, Anacardiaceae; Mediterranean region, photographed in the Padua Botanical Garden, Italy.

Platanus ×acerifolia, London plane tree, Platanaceae; originated in cultivation, photographed on Mainau Island, Lake Constance, Germany.

Platanus ×acerifolia, London plane tree, Platanaceae; originated in cultivation, photographed in the canton of Thurgau, Switzerland.

187

Platanus ×acerifolia, London plane tree, Platanaceae; originated in cultivation, photographed on the Swiss Plateau.

Platanus racemosa, California sycamore, Platanaceae; southwestern North America, photographed in the University of California, Berkeley, Botanical Garden.

Platycladus orientalis, oriental arborvitae, Cupressaceae; eastern Asia, photographed in the Padua Botanical Garden, Italy.

Podocarpus elatus, Australian brown pine, Podocarpaceae; eastern Australia, photographed in the University of California, Berkeley, Botanical Garden.

Platanus orientalis, oriental plane tree, Platanaceae; southwestern
Eurasia, photographed in the Royal Botanic Gardens, Kew, England.

Populus alba, silver poplar, Salicaceae; Eurasia, photographed in the Royal Botanic Gardens, Kew, England.

Populus alba, silver poplar, Salicaceae; Eurasia, photographed in the vicinity of Neuchâtel, Switzerland.

Populus ×*canadensis,* Carolina poplar, Salicaceae; originated in cultivation, photographed in the vicinity of Bienne, Switzerland.

Populus ×*canadensis,* Carolina poplar, Salicaceae; originated in cultivation, photographed in the Royal Botanic Gardens, Kew, England.

Populus ×canadensis 'Robusta', Carolina poplar, Salicaceae; originated
in cultivation, photographed in the Dublin Botanical Garden, Ireland.

Populus ciliata, Himalayan balsam poplar, Salicaceae; Himalaya, photographed in the Royal Botanic Gardens, Kew, England.

Populus deltoides 'Angulata', southern cottonwood, Salicaceae; eastern North America, photographed in the Vallon d'Aubonne Arboretum, Vaud, Switzerland.

Populus lasiocarpa, Chinese necklace poplar, Salicaceae; eastern Asia, photographed in the Munich Botanical Garden, Germany.

Populus nigra, black poplar, Salicaceae; Eurasia, photographed on the Swiss Plateau.

Populus tremula, Eurasian aspen, Salicaceae;
Eurasia, photographed in the Swiss Alps.

Populus tremula, Eurasian aspen, Salicaceae; Eurasia, photographed in the Swiss Alps.

Populus tremuloides, quaking aspen, Salicaceae; North America, photographed in the Rocky Mountains, British Columbia, Canada.

Prunus armeniaca, apricot, Rosaceae; eastern Asia, photographed in the Padua Botanical Garden, Italy.

Prunus avium, mazzard cherry, Rosaceae; western Eurasia, photographed at Mount Usher Gardens, Ireland.

Prunus avium, mazzard cherry, Rosaceae; western Eurasia, photographed in the vicinity of Bienne, Switzerland.

Prunus brigantina, Briançon apricot, Rosaceae; southwestern Europe, photographed in the Padua Botanical Garden, Italy.

Prunus canescens (hoary cherry) × *P. serrula* (birch-bark cherry), Rosaceae; originated in cultivation, photographed in the Hillier Arboretum, England.

Prunus cerasifera, cherry plum, Rosaceae; southwestern Asia, photographed in the Padua Botanical Garden, Italy.

Prunus dulcis, almond, Rosaceae; North Africa, photographed on the Canary Islands, Spain.

Prunus glandulosa 'Sinensis', dwarf flowering almond, Rosaceae; eastern Asia, photographed in the Padua Botanical Garden, Italy.

Prunus laurocerasus, cherry laurel, Rosaceae; southwestern Eurasia, photographed in the Padua Botanical Garden, Italy.

Prunus maackii, Manchurian chokecherry, Rosaceae; eastern Asia, photographed in the Munich Botanical Garden, Germany.

Prunus mahaleb, St. Lucie cherry or mahaleb cherry, Rosaceae; western Eurasia, photographed in the Munich Botanical Garden, Germany.

Prunus sargentii, Sargent cherry, Rosaceae; eastern Asia, photographed in the Royal Botanic Gardens, Kew, England.

Prunus serotina, black cherry, Rosaceae; eastern North America, photographed in the Washington Park Arboretum, Seattle, Washington.

Prunus serrula, birch-bark cherry, Rosaceae; eastern Asia, photographed in the Van Dusen Botanical Garden, Vancouver, Canada.

Prunus serrulata, oriental cherry, Rosaceae; eastern Asia, photographed in the Royal Botanic Gardens, Kew, England.

Prunus serrulata 'Asagi', oriental cherry, Rosaceae; eastern Asia, photographed in the Hillier Arboretum, England.

Prunus serrulata 'Fugenzo', oriental cherry, Rosaceae; eastern Asia, photographed in the Vallon d'Aubonne Arboretum, Vaud, Switzerland.

Prunus ussuriensis, Ussuri cherry, Rosaceae; eastern Asia, photographed in the Royal Botanic Gardens, Kew, England.

Pseudocydonia sinensis, Chinese quince, Rosaceae; eastern Asia, photographed in the Padua Botanical Garden, Italy.

Pseudocydonia sinensis, Chinese quince, Rosaceae; eastern Asia, photographed in the Arboretum des Barres, Nogent-sur-Vernisson, France.

Pseudolarix amabilis, golden larch, Pinaceae; eastern Asia, photographed in the Arboretum des Barres, Nogent-sur-Vernisson, France.

Pseudotsuga menziesii var. *glauca,* Douglas fir, Pinaceae; western North America, photographed in the vicinity of Bienne, Switzerland.

Psidium guajava, guava, Myrtaceae; tropical America, photographed in Costa Rica.

Pterocarya fraxinifolia, Caucasian wing nut, Juglandaceae; southwestern Asia, photographed in a park in Geneva, Switzerland.

Pterocarya stenoptera, Chinese wing nut, Juglandaceae; eastern Asia, photographed in the Royal Botanic Gardens, Kew, England.

Pyrus balansae, Anatolian pear, Rosaceae; southwestern Asia, photographed in the Arboretum des Barres, Nogent-sur-Vernisson, France.

Pyrus calleryana 'Chanticleer', flowering pear, Rosaceae; eastern Asia, photographed in the Van Dusen Botanical Garden, Vancouver, Canada.

Pyrus communis, common pear, Rosaceae; Europe, photographed in the vicinity of Bienne, Switzerland.

Pyrus cordata, Plymouth pear, Rosaceae; western Europe, photographed in the Royal Botanic Gardens, Kew, England.

Pyrus pyrifolia, sand pear, Rosaceae; eastern Asia, photographed in the Royal Botanic Gardens, Kew, England.

Pyrus salicifolia, willow-leaf pear, Rosaceae; southwestern Eurasia, photographed in the Van Dusen Botanical Garden, Vancouver, Canada.

Pyrus ussuriensis, Ussuri pear, Rosaceae; eastern Asia, photographed in the Padua Botanical Garden, Italy.

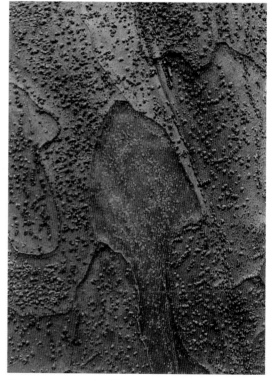

Pyrus ussuriensis, Ussuri pear, Rosaceae; eastern Asia, photographed in the Padua Botanical Garden, Italy.

Quercus acutissima, sawtooth oak, Fagaceae; eastern Asia, photographed in the Royal Botanic Gardens, Kew, England.

Quercus agrifolia, coast live oak, Fagaceae; western North America, photographed by Monterey Bay, California.

Quercus alba, eastern white oak, Fagaceae; eastern North America, photographed in the Royal Botanic Gardens, Kew, England.

Quercus alba, eastern white oak, Fagaceae; eastern North America, photographed in the Royal Botanic Gardens, Kew, England.

Quercus bicolor, swamp white oak, Fagaceae; eastern North America, photographed in the Royal Botanic Gardens, Kew, England.

Quercus canariensis, Algerian oak, Fagaceae; western Mediterranean region, photographed in the Thuret Garden, Cap d'Antibes, France.

Quercus castaneifolia, Persian chestnut oak, Fagaceae; southwestern Asia, photographed in the Royal Botanic Gardens, Kew, England.

Quercus cerris, Turkey oak, Fagaceae; southwestern Eurasia, photographed in the Royal Botanic Gardens, Kew, England.

Quercus frainetto, Hungarian oak, Fagaceae; southwestern Eurasia, photographed in the Arboretum des Barres, Nogent-sur-Vernisson, France.

Quercus frainetto, Hungarian oak, Fagaceae; southwestern Eurasia, photographed in the Royal Botanic Gardens, Kew, England.

Quercus garryana, Oregon white oak, Fagaceae; western North America, photographed in a national forest in Oregon.

Quercus ilex, holm oak, Fagaceae; Mediterranean region, photographed in Cetinale, Tuscany, Italy.

Quercus ithaburensis subsp. *macrolepis*, Vallonea oak, Fagaceae; southwestern Eurasia, photographed in the Royal Botanic Gardens, Kew, England.

Quercus libani, Lebanon oak, Fagaceae; southwestern Asia, photographed in the Royal Botanic Gardens, Kew, England.

Quercus macrocarpa, bur oak, Fagaceae; eastern North America, photographed in the Royal Botanic Gardens, Kew, England.

Quercus mongolica, Mongolian oak, Fagaceae; northeastern Asia, photographed in the Forest Trial Garden, Grafrath, Germany.

Quercus nigra, water oak, Fagaceae; southeastern North America, photographed in the Royal Botanic Gardens, Kew, England.

Quercus petraea, sessile oak, Fagaceae; Europe, photographed in the Royal Botanic Gardens, Kew, England.

Quercus palustris, pin oak, Fagaceae; eastern North America, photographed in the Van Dusen Botanical Garden, Vancouver, Canada.

Quercus pubescens, downy oak, Fagaceae; southwestern Eurasia, photographed in Provence, France.

Quercus robur, English oak, pedunculate oak, Fagaceae; Europe, photographed in a park in Geneva, Switzerland.

Quercus robur, English oak, pedunculate oak, Fagaceae; Europe, photographed on Mainau Island, Lake Constance, Germany.

Quercus rubra, northern red oak, Fagaceae; eastern North America, photographed in the vicinity of Neuchâtel, Switzerland.

Quercus rubra, northern red oak, Fagaceae; eastern North America, photographed on Mainau Island, Lake Constance, Germany.

Quercus suber, cork oak, Fagaceae; Mediterranean region, photographed on the Côte d'Azur, France.

Quercus suber, cork oak, Fagaceae; Mediterranean region, photographed in the Royal Botanic Gardens, Kew, England.

Quercus suber, cork oak, Fagaceae; Mediterranean
region, photographed in Esterel, Côte d'Azur, France.

Quercus ×*turneri,* Turner's oak, Fagaceae; Europe, photographed in the Van Dusen Botanical Garden, Vancouver, Canada.

Quercus velutina, eastern black oak, Fagaceae; eastern North America, photographed in the Royal Botanic Gardens, Kew, England.

Rhamnus hemsleyana, Hemsley buckthorn, Rhamnaceae; eastern Asia, photographed in the Royal Botanic Gardens, Kew, England.

Rhamnus purshiana, cascara buckthorn, Rhamnaceae; western North America, photographed in the Zürich Botanical Garden, Switzerland.

Robinia pseudoacacia, black locust, Leguminosae; eastern North America, photographed
in the vicinity of Bienne, Switzerland.

Salix alba, white willow, Salicaceae; western
Eurasia, photographed in the vicinity of Bienne,
Switzerland.

Salix alba, white willow, Salicaceae; western
Eurasia, photographed in the vicinity of Bienne,
Switzerland.

Salix caprea, goat willow, Salicaceae; Eurasia,
photographed in the Zürich Botanical Garden,
Switzerland.

Salix ×*chrysocoma*, weeping willow, Salicaceae; originated in cultivation, photographed in the vicinity of Neuchâtel, Switzerland.

Salix fragilis, crack willow, Salicaceae; Eurasia, photographed in the vicinity of Bienne, Switzerland.

Sambucus nigra 'Pyramidalis', European black elderberry, Caprifoliaceae; western Eurasia, photographed in the Munich Botanical Garden, Germany.

Sapindus saponaria, soapberry, Sapindaceae; tropical America, photographed in the Orotava Acclimatization Garden, Tenerife, Spain.

Sapium sebiferum, Chinese tallow tree, Euphorbiaceae; eastern Asia, photographed in the Padua Botanical Garden, Italy.

Sassafras albidum, sassafras or mitten tree, Lauraceae; eastern North America, photographed in the Royal Botanic Gardens, Kew, England.

Schinus molle, Peruvian pepper tree, Anacardiaceae; South America, photographed on the Canary Islands, Spain.

Schinus molle, Peruvian pepper tree, Anacardiaceae; South America, photographed on the Canary Islands, Spain.

Sequoia sempervirens, coast redwood, Cupressaceae; western North America, photographed in the Villa Pallavicino Park, Stresa, Italy.

Sequoia sempervirens, coast redwood, Cupressaceae; western North America, photographed in Redwood National Park, California.

Sequoia sempervirens, coast redwood, Cupressaceae; western North America, photographed in northern Italy.

Sequoiadendron giganteum, giant sequoia or big tree, Cupressaceae; western North America, photographed in the vicinity of Bienne, Switzerland.

Sequoiadendron giganteum, giant sequoia or big tree, Cupressaceae; western North America, photographed in the Forest Trial Garden, Grafrath, Germany.

Sophora japonica, Japanese pagoda tree, Leguminosae; eastern Asia, photographed in the vicinity of Bienne, Switzerland.

Sophora japonica, Japanese pagoda tree, Leguminosae; eastern Asia, photographed in the Lausanne Botanical Garden, Switzerland.

Sorbus aria, common whitebeam, Rosaceae; Europe, photographed in the Swiss Jura.

Sorbus aucuparia, rowan, Rosaceae; Europe, photographed in the Swiss Jura.

Sorbus domestica, true service tree, Rosaceae; Mediterranean region, photographed in the Hanbury Garden, La Mortola, Italy.

221

Sorbus domestica f. *pomifera,* round-fruited service tree, Rosaceae; Mediter-ranean region, photographed in the Royal Botanic Gardens, Kew, England.

Sorbus domestica f. *pomifera,* round-fruited service tree, Rosaceae; Mediterranean region, photographed in the Royal Botanic Gardens, Kew, England.

Sorbus hupehensis, Hupeh mountain ash, Rosaceae; eastern Asia, photographed in the Royal Botanic Gardens, Kew, England.

Sorbus latifolia, service tree of Fontainebleau, Rosaceae; Europe, photographed in the Van Dusen Botanical Garden, Vancouver, Canada.

Sorbus torminalis, wild service tree, Rosaceae; Mediterranean region, photographed in the Royal Botanic Gardens, Kew, England.

Stewartia pseudocamellia, Japanese stewartia, Theaceae; eastern Asia,
photographed in the Washington Park Arboretum, Seattle, Washington.

Stewartia pseudocamellia, Japanese stewartia, Theaceae; eastern Asia, photographed in the Royal Botanic Gardens, Kew, England.

Stewartia pteropetiolata var. *koreana,* Korean stewartia, Theaceae; eastern Asia, photographed in the Kalmthout Arboretum, Belgium.

Stewartia sinensis, Chinese stewartia, Theaceae; eastern Asia, photographed in the Royal Botanic Gardens, Kew, England.

Stranvaesia davidiana, stranvaesia, Rosaceae; eastern Asia, photographed in the Hanbury Garden, La Mortola, Italy.

225

Tamarix gallica, French tamarisk, Tamaricaceae; Mediterranean region, photographed in the Padua Botanical Garden, Italy.

Tamarix gallica, French tamarisk, Tamaricaceae; Mediterranean region, photographed in Biarritz, France.

Taxodium distichum, bald cypress, Cupressaceae; southeastern North America, photographed in the Villa Pallavicino Park, Stresa, Italy.

Taxus baccata, English yew, Taxaceae; western Eurasia, photographed in the Zürich Botanical Garden, Switzerland.

Taxodium distichum, bald cypress, Cupressaceae; southeastern North America, photographed in northern Italy.

Thuja plicata, western red cedar, Cupressaceae; western North America, photographed in the Forest Trial Garden, Grafrath, Germany.

Thuja plicata, western red cedar, Cupressaceae; western North America, photographed in the Rocky Mountains, British Columbia, Canada.

Thuja plicata, western red cedar, Cupressaceae; western North America, photographed on the Swiss Plateau.

Thuja standishii, Japanese arborvitae, Cupressaceae; eastern Asia, photographed in the Royal Botanic Gardens, Kew, England.

Thuja standishii, Japanese arborvitae, Cupressaceae; eastern Asia, photographed in the Royal Botanic Gardens, Kew, England.

Tilia americana, basswood or American linden, Tiliaceae; eastern North America, photographed in the Padua Botanical Garden, Italy.

Tilia cordata, little-leaf linden, Tiliaceae; western Eurasia, photographed in the vicinity of Paris, France.

Tilia platyphyllos, big-leaf linden, Tiliaceae; western Eurasia, photographed on the Swiss Plateau.

Tilia platyphyllos 'Rubra', red-twig linden, Tiliaceae; western Eurasia, photographed in the Padua Botanical Garden, Italy.

Tilia ×vulgaris, European linden, Tiliaceae; western Eurasia, photographed in the Swiss Jura.

Torreya nucifera, Japanese nutmeg yew, Taxaceae; eastern Asia, photographed in a park in Geneva, Switzerland.

Torreya nucifera, Japanese nutmeg yew, Taxaceae; eastern Asia, photographed in Montriant Park, Geneva, Switzerland.

Tristaniopsis laurina, Kanuka box or water gum, Myrtaceae; eastern Australia, photographed in the Strybing Arboretum, San Francisco, California.

Tsuga canadensis, eastern hemlock, Pinaceae; northeastern North America, photographed in the Forest Trial Garden, Grafrath, Germany.

Tsuga canadensis, eastern hemlock, Pinaceae; northeastern North America, photographed in the Forest Trial Garden, Grafrath, Germany.

Tsuga diversifolia, northern Japanese hemlock, Pinaceae; eastern Asia, photographed at Fota House, Ireland.

Tsuga heterophylla, western hemlock, Pinaceae; western North America, photographed in the Hoyt Arboretum, Portland, Oregon.

Tsuga mertensiana, mountain hemlock, Pinaceae; western North America, photographed in the Hoyt Arboretum, Portland, Oregon.

Ulmus americana, American white elm, Ulmaceae; eastern North America, photographed in the Washington Park Arboretum, Seattle, Washington.

Ulmus carpinifolia, European field elm, Ulmaceae; Europe, photographed in the Padua Botanical Garden, Italy.

Ulmus carpinifolia, European field elm, Ulmaceae; Europe, photographed in the vicinity of Neuchâtel, Switzerland.

Ulmus glabra, wych elm, Ulmaceae; western Eurasia, photographed in the Swiss Alps.

Ulmus laevis, fluttering elm or European white elm, Ulmaceae; western Eurasia, photographed in the Forest Trial Garden, Grafrath, Germany.

Ulmus pumila, Siberian elm, Ulmaceae; north-eastern Asia, photographed in the Arboretum des Barres, Nogent-sur-Vernisson, France.

Umbellularia californica, California laurel or Oregon myrtle, Lauraceae; western North America, photographed in the Thuret Garden, Cap d'Antibes, France.

Wollemia nobilis, Wollemi pine, Araucariaceae; southeastern Australia, photographed by Wyn G. Jones in Wollemi National Park, Australia, courtesy of Kenneth D. Hill.

Yucca angustissima, narrow-leaf yucca, Agavaceae; southwestern North America, photographed in the Royal Botanic Gardens, Kew, England.

Zelkova carpinifolia, Caucasian elm, Ulmaceae; southwestern Asia, photographed in the Royal Botanic Gardens, Kew, England.

Zelkova serrata, Japanese zelkova, Ulmaceae; eastern Asia, photographed in the Agricultural Experiment Station, Aurora, Washington.

Zelkova sinica, Chinese zelkova, Ulmaceae; eastern Asia, photographed in the Arboretum des Barres, Nogent-sur-Vernisson, France. See also p. 238.

Zelkova carpinifolia, Caucasian elm, Ulmaceae; southwestern Asia, photographed in the Royal Botanic Gardens, Kew, England.

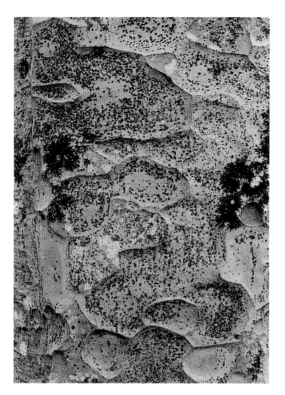

Zelkova sinica, Chinese zelkova, Ulmaceae; eastern Asia, photographed in the Arboretum des Barres, Nogent-sur-Vernisson, France.

Zizyphus jujuba, common jujube or Chinese silver date, Rhamnaceae; Asia, photographed in the Padua Botanical Garden, Italy.

GLOSSARY

The significance of the specialized terminology for bark and related structures and processes is discussed in Chapter 2: Structure, Function & Physical Properties of Bark.

adventitious roots. Roots that emerge from some part of the plant other than a parent root

annular periderm. See continuous periderm

annular rhytidome. Outer bark (rhytidome) that has been produced by a continuous periderm and that peels away from the bark in strings or strips; also known as annular outer bark

assimilates. Substances resulting from photosynthesis and necessary for the structure and function of plants

bark. All the tissues located outside the vascular cambium

bast. See secondary phloem

callose. Substance resembling cellulose that, in the autumn, clogs the conducting elements, usually in an irreversible manner; in a few plants (for example, grapevines, *Vitis*) it can, nevertheless, dissipate in the spring

cambium. See vascular cambium, and cork cambium

companion cells. Thin-walled cells in the phloem that are adjacent to the sieve tube elements and supply them with assimilates

complementary cells. See filling cells

conducting tissue. See vascular tissue

continuous periderm. Secondary protective tissue arranged in the form of rings located in the inner bark; also known as annular periderm

cork. Tissue formed by the cork cambium toward the outside; this tissue is also called phellem or suber independently of whether the cells are suberized or not

cork band. An aggregation of suberized cells making up a vertically oriented band of tissue; this tissue is formed either by enhanced production of cork (true cork bands) or by fragmentation of the rhytidome (false cork bands)

cork cambium. A generally short-lived meristem that is located within the bark, contributing phellem (cork) and phelloderm to the bark; also known as phellogen

cork cell. Any one of several types of cells produced by the cork cambium in the outward direction; also see cork

cortex. A region composed essentially of parenchymatous tissue that is located between the epidermis and the vascular bundles; also known as primary bark

crystals. Deposits within plant cells, generally composed of calcium oxalate or of silicates

dicotyledons. The botanical name for hardwoods (and many other plants); their seedlings have two seed leaves (cotyledons)

dilatation. An expansion of the rays within the bark induced by forces of compression and tension

epidermis. Original protective tissue that covers the parts of the plant located above the soil; it is generally composed of a single layer of cells

f. Abbreviation for the taxonomic rank of form

fascicular cambium. The part of the vascular cambium located within the vascular bundles

fibrovascular bundle. See vascular bundle

filling cells. Masses of parenchyma cells constituting a lenticel and produced by the cork cambium in the position of a former stoma; also known as complementary cells

hard bast. An aggregation of cells in the phloem composed of phloem fibers and having a support function

idioblasts. Individual cells within a tissue that are distinguished from their neighbors by their structure and function

initial periderm. The first periderm formed within the bark

intercellular spaces. Empty spaces between the cells, most commonly at their corners

interfascicular cambium. The part of the vascular cambium located between the vascular bundles

lenticel. Warty aggregation of filling cells (or complementary tissue) produced by the cork cambium; it provides gaseous exchange between the inner bark and the atmosphere and is particularly conspicuous on the bark of cherry (*Prunus*) and birch (*Betula*)

lenticular periderm. Secondary protective tissue, arranged in the form of scales located within the outer bark

liber. Also known as bast; see secondary phloem

lumen. The portion of a cell within the cell wall, usually the hollow space in a dead conducting or support cell

meristem. A living tissue that is capable of cell division; meristems leading to thickening growth (lateral meristems) occur in plants either as a long-lived zone of growth (vascular cambium) or one with a short life (cork cambium)

meristematic. Said of plant cells that are undifferentiated and actively undergo cell divisions

mucilage. Viscous and fluid mixtures of high molecular weight carbohydrates composed of pentosans, hexosans, and derivatives of uric acid

outer bark. See rhytidome

parenchyma cell. Thin-walled cell that can potentially divide

parenchymatous tissue. Aggregation of parenchyma cells

periderm. Secondary protective tissue made up of cork, the cork cambium, and phelloderm

phellem. See cork

phelloderm. Nonsuberized tissue, often rich in chlorophyll, produced by the cork cambium toward the inside

phellogen. See cork cambium

phlobaphene. Amorphous brown coloring matter of the bark

phloem fiber. See sclerenchyma fiber

phloem parenchyma. Storage tissue oriented vertically (axially) in the secondary phloem (bast) and composed of parenchyma cells arranged in bands

phloem ray. Storage tissue oriented radially in the secondary phloem (bast) and composed of parenchyma cells

photosynthesis. Biochemical process within the green parts of plants during which carbon dioxide gas from the air and water from the soil are transformed into sugars (assimilates) using the energy of sunlight

pith. Storage parenchyma located inside the ring of vascular tissue

pore. See vessel

primary bark. See cortex

primary phloem. The first phloem, formed by the procambium toward the outside

primary xylem. The first xylem, produced by the procambium toward the inside

radial section. A vertical cut through a tree trunk that passes through its center, intersecting the rays so that they look like brick walls

resin. Mixture of different derivatives of monoterpenes and sesquiterpenes, retarding decay and microbial activity

rhytidome. Technically, the rhytidome is that part of the bark that lies outside the most recently formed periderm that is still alive; practically, it contains only dead material. Certain trees lack rhytidome; also known as outer bark

rhytidome scale. See scaly rhytidome

scaly periderm. See lenticular periderm

scaly rhytidome. Outer bark (rhytidome) that has been produced by lenticular periderm and that separates from the trunk in flakes, called rhytidome scales; also known as scaly outer bark

sclereids. Sclerenchyma cells with thick, usually lignified cell walls that are sometimes clumped within the bast or in the stalks of fruits. Sclereids can take a variety of shapes: round, elongate, star-shaped, or bone-shaped; also known as stone cells

sclerenchyma. Support tissue within which the cells have uniformly thick walls; two types of cells are distinguished on the basis of their form: the elongate sclerenchyma fibers and the variously shaped sclereids

sclerenchyma fiber. Elongate fiber with a thick, usually lignified wall and functioning for support in the wood (wood fiber and tracheids) and in the bast (phloem fiber)

sclerification. Strengthening of the cells, apparently in response to compression; the cell walls are thickened by deposits of cellulose and lignin

secondary periderm. Any periderm formed after the first one; also known as an additional periderm

secondary phloem. Assimilate conducting tissue within the trunk, formed by the vascular cambium toward the outside; also known as bast or liber

secondary tissues. Any tissues in plants produced by one of the lateral meristems, the vascular cambium or a cork cambium, and leading to a thickening of stems, roots, or leaves

secondary xylem. Water-conducting tissue within the wood, produced by the vascular cambium toward the inside; also known as wood

sieve area. Aggregation of sieve pores in the sieve cells of conifers

sieve cell. The type of sieve element found in conifers

sieve element. Living cell in the phloem with a thin wall, lacking a nucleus, and with a perforated wall in the form of a sieve; within the phloem, it functions primarily in vertical transport of assimilates. Sieve elements of hardwoods are called sieve tube elements; those of conifers are called sieve cells

sieve plate. Aggregation of sieve pores in the end wall of the sieve element of hardwoods

sieve pores. Perforations in the cell walls of sieve elements, permitting the flow of sap from cell to cell. Sieve pores of hardwoods form sieve plates; in conifers, the groups have been called sieve areas

sieve tube element. The type of sieve element found in hardwoods

soft bast. Zones of tissue within the phloem having cells with thin walls (parenchyma cells, companion cells, and sieve elements)

sp. Abbreviation for the taxonomic rank of species

stoma (plural, stomata). Tiny opening in the form of a slit in the epidermis of the green parts of plants, permitting gas exchange

stone cells. See sclereids

suber. See cork

suberin. Fatty acid ester that renders cork cells waterproof when it is deposited in their walls

subsp. Abbreviation for the taxonomic rank of subspecies

tangential section. A vertical cut through a tree trunk that is perpendicular to a line through the center and just grazes the growth rings so that the rays are seen end on

tannins. Chemical substances composed of a mixture of glucose esters of phenolic compounds

tracheids. Water-conducting cells of the xylem in conifers produced by the vascular cambium toward the inside

transverse section. A horizontal cut through a tree trunk that shows the growth rings (when present); also known as a cross section

var. Abbreviation for the taxonomic rank of variety

vascular bundle. Cylinder of conducting tissue composed of xylem, phloem, and in woody plants, of a vascular cambium; also called fibrovascular bundle

vascular cambium. Principal lateral meristem of the tree, with a long life, capable of cell division, and located between the wood and the bark; also known simply as the cambium. It is responsible for the majority of the growth in thickness of a tree through the formation of wood (secondary xylem) and of bast (secondary phloem)

vascular tissue. Tissue that transports water and soluble materials, consisting of xylem and phloem

vessel. Vertical series of lignified cells united into a linked tubular structure of indefinite length that serves to transport water in hardwoods; also known as a pore in transverse sections of the wood

wood. See secondary xylem

wood fiber. Also called libriform fiber; see sclerenchyma fiber

wood parenchyma. Storage tissue oriented vertically in the secondary xylem (wood), composed of parenchyma cells arranged in bands

wood ray. Storage and water-conducting tissue oriented radially in the secondary xylem (wood), composed of parenchyma cells and tracheids

x. Indicates a species of hybrid origin

BIBLIOGRAPHY

The majority of bark studies are found in hundreds of technical articles relating to the structure, properties, and uses of particular kinds of bark. Instead of citing these, here is a selection of books in which the reader can learn more about the structure and function of bark, its uses, and identification.

Boland, D. J., and others. 1984. Forest trees of Australia, ed. 4. CSIRO Publications, East Melbourne. Photographs of bark of about 225 Australian tree species, 24 in color

Cook, G. B. 1961. Cork and the cork tree. Pergamon, Oxford.

Deschênes, H. 1986. Utilization et transformation des bois. Modulo Editeur, Montréal. Includes data on industrial use of bark

Dessain G., and M. Tondelier 1991. Liège de Méditerrannée. Édition Edisud / Narration, Aix-en-Provence. On cork

Esau, K. 1965. Plant anatomy, ed. 2. John Wiley & Sons, New York. Summary treatment of the structure and development of bark, and all other plant parts

Esau, K. 1969. The phloem. Gebrüder Bornträger, Berlin. Very detailed treatment of phloem in all its manifestations in herbaceous plants as well as in trees

Fahn, A. 1974. Plant anatomy, ed. 2. Pergamon, Oxford. Chapters 16 and 17 present a very clear exposition of the development of secondary phloem and of periderm, respectively

Farrar, J. L. 1995. Trees in Canada. Fitzhenry & Whiteside, Toronto. Color photographs of mature bark of 132 northern North American species

Fournier, F., and M. Goulet. 1970. Propriétés physico-mécaniques de l'écorce. Université de Laval, Montréal. Pamphlet emphasizing the material characteristics of bark

Iqbal, M., ed. 1990. The vascular cambium. John Wiley & Sons, New York. Series of individual studies of cambial activities, including production of secondary phloem

Leopold, D. C., W. C. McComb, and R. N. Muller. 1998. Trees of the central hardwood forests of North America. Timber Press, Portland, Oregon. Photographs (some in color) of bark of small, medium, and large trees of some 166 species from central and eastern North America

Little, E. L., Jr. 1980. The Audubon Society field guide to North American trees, eastern region. Alfred A. Knopf, New York. Color photographs of mature bark of 360 species of trees from eastern North America

Little, E. L., Jr. 1980. The Audubon Society field guide to North American trees, western region. Alfred A. Knopf, New York. Color photographs of mature bark of 126 species of trees from western North America

Menninger, E. A. 1967 (reprinted 1995 with a nomenclatural update by J. E. Eckenwalder). Fantastic trees. Timber Press, Portland, Oregon. Black-and-white photographs of trees, illustrating a wide variety of interesting phenomena, many including the bark

Moeller, J. 1882. Anatomie der Baumrinden. Julius Springer, Berlin. Systematic survey of bark structure arranged by families, covering conifers and hardwoods

Oliveira, M. Alves de, and L. de Oliveira. 1991. The cork. Amorim, Lisbon.

Parotta, J. A., J. K. Francis, and R. Rolo de Almeida. 1995. Trees of the Tapajós, a photographic field guide. International Institute of Tropical Forestry, Río Piedras, Puerto Rico. Color photographs of young and old bark of 172 species of Amazonian trees

Philipson, W. R., J. M. Ward, and B. G. Butterfield. 1971. The vascular cambium: its development and activity. Chapman & Hall, London. Brief but effective examination of how wood and bast form

Prance, G. T., and A. E. Prance; photographs by K. B. Sandved. 1993. Bark: the formation, characteristics, and uses of bark around the world. Timber Press, Portland, Oregon. Color photographs of bark in use, on the tree, and as a substrate for various inhabitants, accompanied by a text including many tropical references

Ross, W. D. 1966. Bibliography of bark. Oregon State University, Corvallis. Dated but still useful bibliography for older bark literature

Roth, L., G. Saeger, F. J. Lynch, and J. Weiner. 1960. Structure, extractives, and utilization of bark. Institute of Paper Chemistry, Appleton, Wisconsin. Annotated bibliography of 1339 references emphasizing the practical applications of bark

Rushforth, K. 1999. Trees of Britain and Europe. HarperCollins, London. Color photographs of bark of 350 species of temperate trees cultivated in Great Britain from around the world

Trelease, W. 1931 (reprinted 1967). Winter botany, ed. 3. Dover, New York. Twig characteristics of trees and shrubs native to or cultivated in temperate North America

Van Vliet, A. C. 1971. Converting bark into opportunities. Oregon State University, Corvallis. Discussion of how to make use of all the waste bark generated by the lumber industry

INDEX